Double Delicious!

GOOD, SIMPLE FOOD FOR BUSY, COMPLICATED LIVES

Jessica Seinfeld

Photographs by **LISA HUBBARD** • Illustrations by **STEVE VANCE**

Design by **3&Co.**

Produced by **SMALLWOOD & STEWART, INC.**

Published by

WM

WILLIAM MORROW

An Imprint of HarperCollinsPublishers

HarperCollins books may be purchased for educational, business, or sales promotional use. For information, please write: Special Markets Department, HarperCollins Publishers, 10 East 53rd Street, New York, NY 10022.

Illustrations © 2010 Steve Vance
Photographs © 2010 Lisa Hubbard
Food styling: Ann Disrude
Prop styling: Deborah Williams
First Edition
This book was produced by
Smallwood & Stewart, Inc.
5 East 20th Street, New York, NY 10003
www.smallwoodandstewart.com

Design by 3&Co.
www.threeandco.com

Library of Congress Cataloging-in-Publication data is available upon request.

ISBN 978-0-06-165933-1

10 11 12 13 14   10 9 8 7 6 5 4 3 2 1

To my grandmother, Eleanor, who is still

brilliant and beautiful at age 97

Contents

BREAKFAST

MEALTIME

DESSERT

ESSENTIALS

Introduction

As a parent of three young children, one of my biggest daily challenges is helping them with the habits, attitudes, and orientation toward food that will carry them through life. Before I had kids, I thought that would be simple. I have always loved to cook, and I grew up eating fresh vegetables and fruits, so I naively thought they would love the same healthy foods as me.

How wrong I was.

To my shock and dismay, putting good food in front of them not only didn't work, it often put their eating habits into reverse. As hard as I tried to make cute-looking, "fun" meals, and to chop vegetables into teeny, tiny pieces, these were ultimately labor-intensive and unsuccessful meals. In fact, there were countless meals where it seemed as if my older two children ate next to nothing. I was really worried that they were not getting the right nutrients; at the same time, I also worried that stress and high pressure around the table would make matters worse, both for the short and long term. Pretty soon, food fatigue and frustration settled in and I realized that I had to find alternatives.

Then came my first personal breakthrough: vegetable purees—

a time-honored device that worked wonders with my kids through the nonintimidating foods they already loved. That little personal triumph became the impetus for my book *Deceptively Delicious.*

But even after my initial progress, I knew there was more to nutrition and healthful eating than just pureed veggies. And like all things concerning my children, I wanted to do more for them. So I continued my food adventure: a search for more healthy options, fresh and rich ingredients, and always—ALWAYS—delicious flavor. This book is the result of that adventure.

NOT-SO-SUPER MARKETS

Wouldn't it be great if supermarkets and food companies placed the same priority as parents do on making life simple and healthy? But the food industry and parents are on different missions. This became clear to me as I started to look for nutritional answers and strategies in the grocery store, and I was quickly overwhelmed by a sea of confusing packages and conflicting labels.

I'm sure you know the dilemma. You're staring at a wall of breakfast cereals. Each colorful box is screaming its nutritional claims at you: Vitamins! Fiber! Grains! Low-fat! Cholesterol free! Trans-fat-free! Heart-healthy! They all claim to be good for you—even the ones you KNOW are not.

Food and ingredient decisions are more difficult than ever. Companies that make food misrepresent or mislead us into buying products with little or no nutritional value. Stores that sell food will sometimes try to strategically lead us toward the least healthy food options. And each publication we read brings us an overload of nutritional studies, all contradicting something we've just read somewhere else.

What are you supposed to believe? Which health claims are real, and which are there to trick you? How can you get back to food basics, build a manageable, healthy lifestyle, and make sure you are making the right choices for you and your family?

CRACKING THE CODE

The answer for me was education and taking small steps.

First, I started reading everything I could get my hands on and spoke to nutritional experts like Joy Bauer. Once

I realized what the problems were, the answers became obvious. And for me, a little education and a lot of perseverance have gone a long way.

Then, once I had a plan to improve my family's eating habits, I followed the advice of food and nutrition professionals such as New York University professor Lisa Sasson, who introduced me to simple ways of getting more nutritious foods into my family. She taught me how to shop for food wisely. Along the way, I learned that suddenly changing the way your family eats is pretty close to impossible. Instead, the incremental changes I have made have meant that my family was not forced or shocked into eating food that looked and tasted different from what they were used to.

Slowly but surely, I have gotten the Seinfelds from point A (very simple foods that contain few nutrients) to point B (foods that are full of good things, including veggies and whole grains). And I have discovered that the benefits of good, healthy food go beyond the well-being of each individual. Good food makes us a happy and harmonious family. How, you ask? When you feed your family good food, I assure you, you will feel like you are doing a great job as a parent. Moreover, you don't have to pressure them to eat everything—because even

if they skip some things, you know the next meal they eat at home will be nutritious, too. It makes for a relaxed and enjoyable mealtime.

FOOD MATH!
ADDITION WITHOUT SUBTRACTION

If you read my first book, you know that I believe in finding ways to make ordinary foods extraordinary by loading them up with healthy ingredients, such as pureed vegetables and fruits.

But while fruits and vegetables are important, there are many other simple, healthy ingredients that you can add to make everyday food even better. I'll share with you some delicious ways to add whole grains to your baked goods, boost sweetness without a lot of sugar, and make luxurious sauces without artery-clogging fats. You don't even have to take my word that these recipes are good for you! At the bottom of each recipe we've added a simple nutritional analysis by Joy Bauer so you can see how many calories or how little fat is in each dish. And just as before, it's not about making "health food." It's about making the food you eat do more for your body and making it even more delicious.

PEACE, LOVE, AND HEALTHY INGREDIENTS

In the pages ahead, you'll find a whole new array of family favorites—breakfasts, lunches, dinners, snacks, and treats—improved by adding in the healthy nutrients that we all need.

Not only are these recipes delicious and good for us, but, with a few exceptions, they're quick and easy to make, too. We all lead busy lives and don't have a lot of extra time to spend in the kitchen. So the majority of recipes in this book don't require a lot of prep time and could even be made by someone with limited cooking experience. As I was developing them I kept thinking, "Can Ally handle this?" (she is my dear friend who is just learning how to cook), and "Can Rebecca find time to make this?" (that's my sister who has 4 young kids as well as another full-time job). Recipes that have a special tab that says "Quick" require just 20 minutes or less of hands-on prep time, after which you can leave everything to cook.

These recipes are the result of lots of experimentation. I'm always trying, failing, refining, and improving. Along the way, I create plenty of culinary disasters. Believe me, I know what doesn't work. But after many kitchen disasters (like green chocolate-chip cookies, hot-pink spaghetti sauce, and bread so tough you could bounce it against the wall) and many more triumphs, I realized food can be fun and easy to prepare, delicious and satisfying to eat, and a rewarding source of fulfillment that comes from doing something great for the people you love the most. In the pages ahead, I hope you'll find that the recipes and tips that really work for my family's health and happiness work for yours as well.

Let's get started!

Meet the Kitchen Cabinet

Jessica

I am very pleased to introduce you to my Kitchen Cabinet—my husband, Jerry, my three children, and nutritionist Joy Bauer. While everyone who eats at my home—friends and family—is part of the review panel, it's my husband and children who I trust most to advise and help me taste (and retaste) all of the recipes in this book. If you read *Deceptively Delicious*, you have already been introduced. But two years is a long time, particularly in the life of a child, so let's get caught up.

Sascha

Our oldest child, and only daughter, is nine. I knew Sascha was going to make things interesting for us when she spit out peas in her high chair the first time I gave them to her when she was a few months old. As she has grown, she has gotten a bit better about trying new foods. Being in the kitchen preparing her own snacks and cooking with me has definitely helped. But she is a nibbler at best, eating only little bits of food at a time—except when it comes to dessert. Somehow, her appetite then gets much bigger.

Julian

Our middle child is seven years old and a voracious eater. Julian will eat a nice, robust meal without any prodding, and he is often up for seconds. He is curious but cautious about new foods. He first likes to smell new foods he is trying. Then he has a little lick, a tiny nibble, until finally, almost always, a smile appears and he announces, "It's good!!" to the table.

Shepherd

Our "baby" is no longer a baby! He is five years old and has no issues with food. He reaches for broccoli and sweet potatoes on his plate first! Easy breezy. Much to the amazement of Sascha and Julian, he just likes all foods! Shepherd is his own man and could not care less what his siblings like or don't like. In fact, there is nothing he won't try.

Jerry

My loving husband is the best eater in the house. He eats and enjoys anything I make. He is also a great dessert taster. No matter how full he is, he will always try something and give me a very honest answer. He is a big late-night snacker, so I have to hide treats I am working on from him. He is generally a healthy and disciplined eater but he definitely knows how to let loose (hence the cinnamon buns named for him in this book).

Joy

Joy is our VERY stringent recipe vetter. She makes sure I stick to ingredients that are low in fat and sodium and that are nutritionally dense as well. Not every recipe passed muster with Joy, because in my reality, sometimes perfect nutrition must be passed over for superquick and efficient. But for the most part, everything in this book will keep you on track, if you do your part by keeping your portions in check.

Shopping Healthfully & Wisely

AN AISLE-BY-AISLE GUIDE TO YOUR GROCERY STORE

It all starts with smart shopping. Without the right ingredients in the house, it's hard to eat well. Unfortunately, choosing the right ingredients and products is not that simple—if it were, wouldn't we all be healthy and fit?

Instead, when faced with hundreds of products on the supermarket shelves—many outright unhealthy and some masquerading as healthy—smart shopping becomes almost like a search-and-rescue mission. To make healthy, nutritious choices, we, the weary and often child-toting shopper, must not be distracted or misled, and must focus on separating the good from the bad. We need to stay alert and think like a food scientist.

Alas, thinking like a scientist doesn't come naturally to many of us, certainly not to me, so I turned to my friend Lisa Sasson, a nutritionist in the Department of Nutrition, Food Studies, and Public Health at New York University, to help me develop some guidelines for selecting more nutritious foods—in nearly every part of the store—aisle by aisle. It has become my personal road map to the grocery store and has made shopping faster, easier, and healthier. I hope you'll find it helpful, too.

Know Your Food Label

The food label that appears on everything from bottled water to breakfast cereal reveals more about what you're buying than any of the more prominent claims on the front of the package. Use it to compare products, discover what they truly contain, and check for allergens so you can make healthier choices.

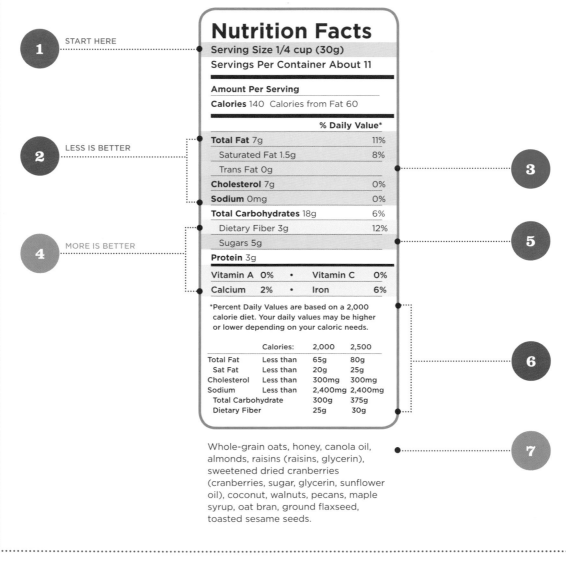

1 — START HERE

2 — LESS IS BETTER

4 — MORE IS BETTER

Nutrition Facts

Serving Size 1/4 cup (30g)

Servings Per Container About 11

Amount Per Serving

Calories 140 Calories from Fat 60

	% Daily Value*
Total Fat 7g	11%
Saturated Fat 1.5g	8%
Trans Fat 0g	
Cholesterol 7g	0%
Sodium 0mg	0%
Total Carbohydrates 18g	6%
Dietary Fiber 3g	12%
Sugars 5g	
Protein 3g	

Vitamin A	0%	Vitamin C	0%
Calcium	2%	Iron	6%

*Percent Daily Values are based on a 2,000 calorie diet. Your daily values may be higher or lower depending on your caloric needs.

	Calories:	2,000	2,500
Total Fat	Less than	65g	80g
Sat Fat	Less than	20g	25g
Cholesterol	Less than	300mg	300mg
Sodium	Less than	2,400mg	2,400mg
Total Carbohydrate		300g	375g
Dietary Fiber		25g	30g

3

5

6

7

Whole-grain oats, honey, canola oil, almonds, raisins (raisins, glycerin), sweetened dried cranberries (cranberries, sugar, glycerin, sunflower oil), coconut, walnuts, pecans, maple syrup, oat bran, ground flaxseed, toasted sesame seeds.

1. **Serving size.** Calories and nutrients on the label are listed **per serving**. But serving sizes are usually smaller than you think. Very often you'll consume more than one serving, so increase the nutrients and calories proportionately.

2. **Look for a low (5% or less) Percent Daily Values for fat, saturated fat, cholesterol, and sodium.** Most of us eat too much of these things. Diets high in these nutrients can increase your risk of heart disease and high blood pressure.

3. **Trans fat.** You may also see the term "partially hydrogenated fat." This type of fat is said to do the most damage to our arteries. It's found in cakes, cookies, fried foods, salad dressings, snack foods, and stick margarines. Look for products that are "trans-fat-free."

4. **Look for a high (20% or more) Percent Daily Values for dietary fiber, vitamin A, vitamin C, calcium, and iron (especially for children, teens, and postmenopausal women).** Eating adequate amounts of these nutrients can improve your health and may reduce your risk of certain chronic diseases. No one food has a high Percent Daily Values for every nutrient, so a varied diet is essential.

5. **Sugars.** There is no recommendation for the amount of sugar to eat per day. Sugars on the label include naturally occurring ones (those found in fruits and milk) and added sugars such as corn syrup, high-fructose corn syrup, fruit juice concentrate, molasses, maltose, dextrose, sucrose, brown sugar, invert sugar, raw sugar, turbinado, honey, and maple syrup. It's not good to consume too much added sugar, regardless of the source.

6. **Recommended daily intake numbers.** Nutrients that have upper limits, such as fat, cholesterol, and sodium, are listed first. The lower limit of other nutrients, such as fiber, are listed next, meaning we should eat *at least* this amount per day. Bear in mind these figures are based on a 2,000-calorie and 2,500-calorie diet, which covers most adult females and males, respectively. Our individual calorie requirements differ greatly depending on many factors—principally age, activity level, and gender.

7. **Ingredients are listed by weight, from highest to lowest.**

BOTTOM LINE

I try to stay away from products with a long list of ingredients, especially those with lots of added sugars, high sodium, or trans fats.

Fruits & Vegetables

It's safe to say we all need to eat more vegetables and fruits: They're an essential part of a good diet. We also need to eat a variety of them to make sure we get the full benefits nutritionally. Fortunately, nature has done its own labeling: The different colors of fruits and vegetables actually indicate the presence of different nutrients. So, simply combining as many colors as possible in your basket ensures a good mix.

Besides mixing colors, go for in-season produce, ideally locally grown. Not only does it taste better but it's likely to be fresher and have more nutrients. Strawberries or corn may look enticing in midwinter but after the long transport and storage, the nutrients and flavors will probably have diminished significantly.

Out of season, consider frozen produce, which can have even more nutrients than fresh, because they've been flash frozen at their peak. And of course, frozen fruits and vegetables need less preparation in the kitchen—purees take half the time!

Canned pumpkin, sweet potato, and tomato products are also good options out of season. With any frozen or canned food, look at the label and avoid those with added salt, sugars, or fats.

What I Buy...

Vegetables: Buy whatever is in season and looks fresh. Broccoli, bell peppers (all colors), okra, carrots, tomatoes, squash, and dark, leafy greens such as spinach or collard greens are among the most nutritious choices.

Fruits: Again, choose whatever is in season and fresh. Top choices nutritionally include: blackberries, blueberries, strawberries, raspberries, oranges, bananas, watermelon, apples, melon, pink grapefruit, pomegranate, grapes, cherries, kiwi, and mangoes.

Fresh herbs: Herbs, like basil, mint, rosemary, and sage, contribute added aroma and flavors that can reduce the amount of salt we use. They can also be a good source of vitamins, minerals, and phytochemicals (substances found naturally in plant foods that promote health and reduce the risk of disease).

Dried fruits: I like to use dried fruits, like raisins, apricots, and prunes, to add natural sweetness to foods or to eat as a snack on the run. They're good sources of vitamins, minerals, and fiber. But because they're so concentrated, watch portion size, as calories can quickly add up.

Make sure dried fruit does not have added sugars or oils—check the label! Also, be aware that the concentrated natural sugars in dried fruit can contribute to tooth decay. A quick rinse with water, a tooth-brushing, or even chewing sugar-less gum cuts down on risk of decay.

Dairy

Dairy products are rich in calcium, protein, and vitamins. Not surprisingly, fat is the problem here. The good news is that skim milk or 1% low-fat milk provide all the same nutrition with little or no fat. So, go for low-fat options in this aisle and watch out for products that say they're low-fat but have long ingredients lists, like some yogurts, creamers, and whipped toppings. For sour cream and frozen yogurt, where a little fat may be necessary for flavor and texture, reduced fat can be a tastier option than low-fat or non-fat.

What I Buy...

Milk: Most health authorities agree that children under 2 years should drink whole milk, but for everyone else, low-fat (1%) or non-fat (skim) milk is a much better alternative. In case you're wondering, there is a big difference between 1%, 2%, and full-fat milk: 1% milk has less than half the fat of 2% (and a quarter that of whole milk)!

If you are getting away from dairy-based milk altogether, try unsweetened soy or rice milk (with calcium and vitamin D added). They taste better than you might think!

Low-fat sour cream: Low-fat sour cream contains half the fat of regular, and I'll bet you can't tell the difference when it's used on a potato or in a dip.

Low-fat Greek yogurt: Yogurt should have only a couple of ingredients and little or no added sugars and no artificial sweeteners. I prefer Greek yogurt because even the low-fat or fat-free varieties are creamier than most regular yogurts and they contain up to 50% more protein.

Look for yogurts with live, active cultures, which may aid digestion.

Trans-fat-free soft tub margarine:
Soft (tub) or liquid margarines have less hydrogenated fat than stick and about a quarter of the saturated fat of most butters.

A little butter every so often is fine. What I don't use, I wrap well and freeze to preserve freshness as long as possible. The most important thing is to use it sparingly.

Low-fat cheese: When topping a pizza or tucked in a quesadilla, low-fat cheese is a perfectly good substitute with less than half the fat of a typical cheese. When it's the "star," such as part of an hors d'oeuvre, I'll choose a really delicious full-fat cheese and serve it in small quantities.

Low-fat buttermilk: Low-fat (1%) buttermilk contains less than half the fat of whole milk, yet has all the richness of flavor. I use it to make mashed potatoes or salad dressings creamy or to add moisture to pancakes, cakes, and muffins.

Eggs: Check the date on the carton. It is considered safe to use eggs four to five weeks after their "sell by" date, but I don't recommend it. The taste and quality of the egg diminish over time. The color of eggs, brown or white, makes no difference nutritionally.

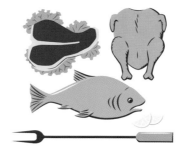

Meat, Poultry & Fish

Go for lean cuts of meat and white-meat poultry, then trim the excess fat and remove the skin from chicken before cooking. Look for meat cuts labeled as "lean" or "extra-lean."

Even with lean cuts, portion control is important. It is recommended that most adults consume no more than 6 ounces of lean meat, poultry or fish a day—that's a piece only about the size of 2 decks of cards.

The American Heart Association recommends eating some variety of fish twice a week. It is a rich source of protein and many vitamins and minerals, and has omega-3 fatty acids (see page 199), which appear to protect the heart. Most store-bought fish is farm raised; a better option is wild fish, if it is available and affordable. It is healthier, has more flavor, and is better for the environment.

Everyone, especially children and pregnant women, should avoid fish with high levels of mercury, such as shark, swordfish, tilefish, and king mackerel. These fish should be consumed sparingly by anyone. A good site for information on mercury in fish is epa.gov/waterscience/fish/states.htm.

What I Buy...

Beef: Look for the word "round" or "loin" in the name of the cut, such as tenderloin or top round; flank steak is also good. These are the leanest cuts. If you're choosing ground beef select 90% lean.

Pork: Loin cuts, such as tenderloin, loin chop, and loin roast, are the leanest cuts, as well as ham.

Chicken and Turkey: Choose skinless breast, or remove the skin before cooking. Ground poultry—turkey or chicken breast—is a great low-fat alternative to ground beef for burgers and meat sauces.

Nitrate-free or extra-lean Turkey Bacon: This is my choice when I absolutely must have the flavor of bacon.

Fish: Good options are canned light tuna, smaller fish (which have lower mercury), and shellfish. Look for anchovies, catfish, clams, flounder, pollack, salmon, sardines, shrimp, scallops, tilapia, trout, or whitefish.

Oils

Whenever possible, I use an oil-based cooking spray to provide all the fat I need to cook with and no more. Canola oil or olive oil are good choices when I don't use a spray.

Proper storage is important to preserve the nutritional benefits and flavor of oils. Exposure to oxygen, heat, and light can cause them to go rancid. Purchase or transfer oils to glass or metal containers—the darker the better. Store in a dark, cool cabinet (not over the stove as I used to do!) and buy in small amounts.

What I Buy...

Canola oil: Canola oil is one of the healthier cooking oils, with more heart healthy omega-3 fatty acids (see page 199) than other vegetable oils. Because it's flavorless it can be used in any number of ways.

Extra-virgin olive oil: Extra-virgin olive oil is from the first pressing of olives, so it is the least handled and retains the most nutrient properties. Nutritionists say that olive oil contains active biological compounds that may help reduce the incidence of some chronic diseases, such as cancer and heart disease.

Breads & Cereals

There are a lot of confusing health claims made on bread and breakfast cereal packaging. Regardless, the ingredients list is where you'll discover the true contents—not on the front of the package. Look for a "whole" grain as a first ingredient, such as whole wheat. Whole-grain products contain the whole kernel, which is rich in fiber, vitamins, minerals, and other active compounds that may help reduce the risk of heart disease, diabetes, and cancer. Grains that are "refined" have these parts of the kernel removed and lose the most important nutrients. Breads that claim to be "made with" whole wheat, wheat, multigrain, seven grain, and/or stoned wheat, are probably made from mostly refined, not whole grains.

Most breakfast cereals, even some made with whole grains, contain a lot of added sugars. If sugar, high-fructose corn syrup, dextrose, maple sugar, etc., appears high up in the ingredients list, find another option! I prefer to sweeten my own cereal with fresh or dried fruit rather than have the manufacturer do it. Also, I don't buy any cereal that uses artificial food coloring.

Granola cereals always look and sound healthy, but they can be high in fat and calories and may contain some hydrogenated fats. I look for low-fat granola or make my own (see page 29).

Finally, check portion size when comparing breakfast cereals. The nutritional analysis on the side of the box is for a modest ½–1 cup serving. Most of us take much more. I use a measuring cup every time I pour a bowl for myself.

What I Buy...

Whole-grain breads: Look for "whole grain" or "whole wheat" as the first ingredient and check out the grams of fiber. Breads that are good sources of fiber have around 3 grams per slice (recommended daily fiber intake for adults is 25 to 35 grams.)

Breakfast cereals: Choose cereals with at least 3 grams of fiber per serving and low sugar—the sugar content of a single serving can range from 0 to 21 grams (4 grams is a teaspoonful)!

Pasta, Rice, Beans & Grains

Beans and grains are among the healthiest and most versatile foods you can find. They're good sources of protein, fiber, vitamins, phytochemicals, and minerals; they're an excellent, inexpensive substitute for meat; and best of all, they're satisfying without adding a lot of calories.

Look for whole-grain products first. If the product has "enriched" on the label, it means the grain is refined with some vitamins and minerals added back during processing. Whole grains naturally have no (or very little) salt, provide heart

healthy unsaturated fat (although very little), and are good sources of fiber.

My family loves pasta so I'm happy we've made the switch to whole-wheat varieties, which have all the nutritional benefits of any whole-grain product. How long you cook pasta matters a lot and in fact, the experts say that it actually affects its nutritional value. They say pasta is best cooked *al dente* (which translates as "to the bite") so that it's slightly firm.

Like oils, brown rice and other whole-grains can go rancid, losing their nutritional value as well as their flavor. So buy them in small quantities, find a dark, cool cupboard for short-term storage (up to a couple of months), and keep whole-grain flours in the freezer for longer periods.

What I Buy...

Whole-wheat pasta: Switching to whole-wheat or multigrain pasta is one of the simplest and quickest ways to increase your family's fiber intake (whole-wheat has up to three times the fiber of regular pasta). I made the switch by serving half regular and half whole-wheat pasta together, and slowly moving to all whole-wheat.

Brown rice: Nuttier and chewier than regular white rice, brown rice is also higher in fiber and vitamin E. Again, you can introduce it slowly, gradually mixing it in with regular rice.

Oatmeal: Oatmeal is one of my favorite grains, and can be so much more than a delicious breakfast. It's great for cookies and as a topping in cakes, pies, and crumbles.

Quinoa (pronounced *keen-wah*): Like kasha, wild rice, barley, and wheat berries, quinoa is rich in protein, vitamins, and minerals and high in fiber. Quinoa is actually a mild-flavored seed that cooks like rice, but much faster. Use it in soups, as a substitute for rice, or as a hot cereal (see page 30).

Whole-wheat flour: Whole-wheat flour will boost the fiber in your diet and add all the health benefits of whole grains. In doughs or batters, whole-wheat flour can replace refined white flour or all-purpose flour. Because whole-wheat flour can make baked goods too dense, I'll often mix whole-wheat and all-purpose flour.

Flaxseed: I use flaxseed a lot, sprinkling it on cereal or yogurt or adding it to bread crumb toppings or in baked goods, because it's a really good source of omega-3 fatty acids and fiber. In its whole form, flaxseed is less susceptible to spoilage, but should be ground before use so you can absorb it more easily. Store whole flaxseed in a dark container

in a cool place; ground flaxseed should be stored in the refrigerator or, better still, kept in the freezer.

Canned beans: Most canned beans have added salt, so I rinse them a few times or use dried. Preparing dried beans is easy, but it does take time: Soak the beans around eight hours or overnight, then drain the water a couple of times (which helps to make them less gassy). Then cook them for 1–4 hours, depending on the bean, until they are tender.

Juices & Sodas

Since they were little, I've tried to train my kids not to expect something sweet to satisfy their thirst. So the drink of choice for my family is filtered tap water or bottled water, when necessary. Juice is considered a special treat on occasion. We have lots of fun making our own freshly squeezed orange juice. I use an electric citrus juicer, which you can find for less than twenty dollars online, to make pure homemade juices.

If I buy juice, I look for 100% fruit or vegetable juice. To be real juice, fruits or vegetables should be the only ingredients.

Check drinks closely that say they are "made with real fruit"—they may actually contain very little real fruit juice and lots of added sugars and, quite often, artificial coloring. The word "drink" on the label also probably signifies that it is made with something other than 100% juice.

Also, remember that all juices—and, of course, all sodas—contain sugar, so they can contribute to tooth decay. Carbonated soft drinks, fruit drinks, punches, fruit ades, sweetened teas, and coffee drinks are usually high in added sugars and calories with little if any nutritional benefits. Many commercially made smoothies also fall into this category.

What I Buy...

Juice: If you buy juice boxes, make sure they are the small 4-ounce size and that they are 100% juice. According to the American Academy of Pediatrics, *daily* juice consumption for 1- to 6-year-olds should be limited to 4–6 ounces and to 8–12 ounces for 7- to 18-year-olds.

Snacks

I am sorry to break the news, but no matter what the label says, snack foods will not contribute significant amounts of healthy nutrients to your diet. They're meant to be tasty. Regardless of what the label boasts, snack foods are treats—that means they are to be enjoyed on occasion and in moderation.

The thing that dooms much of our snacking is portion size. Even small bags that look like a single portion are often more—sometimes 3 times more! Try buying individual-serving bags, or buy in bulk and then portion it out yourself in small sandwich bags. Snacks packaged in "single serving" sizes make it harder to overeat.

And, as always, read the label carefully. There are some low-fat options, but be aware that although the label may advertise "low-fat" or "trans-fat-free," the product can still be high in added sugars and/or calories and sodium.

Almost everybody buys potato chips from time to time. Regular chips have around 9–10 grams of total fat per serving; reduced-fat chips, with about half that amount, are a better option.

Baked chips do have less fat, but to me it all comes down to taste. I prefer to eat fewer regular chips to satisfy my craving for something savory and crunchy, rather than eating more of some overly processed baked chips, which may still leave me with the same craving!

Vegetable chips may sound nutritious—and look pretty—but nutritionally they are not much different than regular chips. Most of the vegetables' nutrition is washed, deep fried, and processed away.

What I Buy...

Cookies: When choosing cookies, buy the simplest ones you can find. They tend to have fewer calories and fewer unhealthy ingredients. I buy whole-wheat graham crackers, Bunny or Teddy Grahams, ginger snaps, and fruit bars.

Granola and cereal bars: I look for products made with whole grains, then select those with low calories and high fiber. Lots of these bars, particularly so-called energy bars, contain many types of sugars and syrups and are similar in nutrition to candy bars—with some vitamins and minerals sprinkled in. I try to choose granola or cereal bars that have around 130 calories or less per bar. Clif Z Bars for kids are popular in the Seinfeld home (I remind everyone to brush their teeth afterward!)

Pretzels: Pretzels should have no fat and only a few ingredients. Stay away from those that have added fats and flavorings.

Nuts and Seeds: Almonds, cashews, sunflower seeds, pumpkin seeds, walnuts, and peanuts are good sources of vitamins, minerals, phytochemcials, fiber, and heart-healthy fats. Although rich in nutrients, all nuts and seeds are high in calories, so eat in moderation. I look for nuts and seeds that do not have added salt, sugars, flavorings, or oils.

Breakfast

Crunchy Almond Granola

QUICK!

Prep:
5 minutes

Total:
35 minutes

Yield:
Serves 8

Store-bought granolas can be loaded with saturated fat and sugar. I developed my own that's healthier (and I think tastier). It's addictive, so I pre-measure ½ cup servings in baggies to ensure portion control!

- ¼ cup sesame seeds
- ¼ cup flaxseed meal
- ¼ cup raw almonds
- ¼ cup raw cashews
- ¼ cup raisins
- ¼ cup dates, chopped
- ½ cup bran cereal, such as Nature's Path Smart Bran
- 1 cup unsweetened crispy brown rice cereal, such as Erewhon Crispy Brown Rice Cereal
- 1 cup old-fashioned oats
- 1 teaspoon cinnamon
- ¼ cup honey
- ½ cup **carrot puree**

1. Preheat the oven to 350°F.

2. Combine all the ingredients in a large bowl.

3. Spread evenly onto a greased baking sheet. Bake for 30 minutes, stirring occasionally to prevent overbrowning. Let cool. Store in an airtight container or zipper-lock plastic bag.

Julian:
This is my dad's favorite breakfast cereal.

Shepherd:
Mine too!

Calories: 209, Carbohydrate: 36 g, Protein: 5 g, Total Fat: 7 g, Saturated Fat: 1 g, Sodium: 35 mg, Fiber: 6.5 g

Prep:
20 minutes

Total:
20 minutes

Yield:
Serves 6

Cinnamon-Maple Quinoa

Quinoa is one of those super-healthy foods that's so delicious and easy to prepare, you wonder why we don't eat it more often. Packed with protein, fiber, and minerals, it makes a great comfy and cozy (gluten-free) breakfast.

- 1¼ cups water
- 1 cup quinoa
- 1 tablespoon trans-fat-free soft tub margarine spread
- ½ cup **sweet potato puree**
- 1 tablespoon pure maple syrup
- ⅓ cup light vanilla soy milk or nonfat (skim) milk
- ¼ teaspoon cinnamon
- Pinch of salt
- 6 teaspoons pure maple syrup, divided for garnish
- 6 teaspoons chopped walnuts or almonds, divided for garnish

1. In a small saucepan, bring the water to a boil. Meanwhile, rinse the quinoa in cold water and strain. Add the quinoa to the boiling water and reduce heat to a simmer. Cook for 12 minutes, uncovered. Remove the pot from the heat, cover, and let sit for 5 minutes.

2. In a separate pot, melt the margarine. Stir in the sweet potato puree, 1 tablespoon of the maple syrup, soy milk, cinnamon, and salt. When the quinoa has finished cooking, stir in the sweet potato mixture. Divide into bowls and top with a teaspoon each of maple syrup and nuts.

Joy:
Though it's considered a whole grain, quinoa is actually a protein-rich seed. It makes a great alternative to oatmeal in the morning.

Calories: 186, Carbohydrate: 30 g, Protein: 5.5 g, Total Fat: 5 g, Saturated Fat: 0.5 g, Sodium: 100 mg, Fiber: 3 g

Maple Spice Muffins

You simply can't go wrong with maple and allspice. At least in our house you can't. My husband actually claims that "this is what heaven smells like."

Shown here with Jerry's Cinnamon Buns (recipe p. 34).

Shown here with Jerry's Cinnamon Buns (recipe p. 34).

QUICK!

Prep:
20 minutes

Total:
50 minutes

Yield:
Makes 12 muffins

- Nonstick cooking spray
- ¼ cup trans-fat-free soft tub margarine spread
- ½ cup pure maple syrup
- 1 (6-ounce) container of low-fat lemon yogurt
- ½ cup nonfat sour cream
- 1 large egg
- 1 large carrot, washed and grated
- 1 small apple, grated
- ½ cup raisins
- 1 cup all-purpose flour
- 1 cup whole-wheat pastry flour
- 1 teaspoon baking soda
- 1 teaspoon baking powder
- 1½ teaspoons cinnamon
- 1 teaspoon allspice
- ½ teaspoon ground clove
- ¼ teaspoon salt

1. Preheat the oven to 350°F. Coat a 12-cup muffin tin with cooking spray or line with paper baking cups.

2. In a large bowl, stir the margarine, maple syrup, yogurt, sour cream, egg, carrot, apple, and raisins, breaking up the margarine with a spoon.

3. Sprinkle the 2 types of flour, baking soda, baking powder, cinnamon, allspice, clove, and salt over the margarine mixture. Stir until just combined, but do not overmix—the batter is supposed to be lumpy.

4. Divide the batter among the muffin cups. Bake until the tops of the muffins are lightly browned and a toothpick comes out clean when inserted into the center, 20 to 25 minutes. Turn the muffins out onto a rack to cool.

5. Store in an airtight container at room temperature for up to 2 days, or wrap individually and freeze for up to 1 month.

Shepherd:
Does heaven really smell like cinnamon?

1 serving = 1 muffin
Calories: 198, Carbohydrate: 35 g, Protein: 4 g, Total Fat: 5 g, Saturated Fat: 1 g, Sodium: 250 mg, Fiber: 2.5 g

Prep:
1 hour 45 minutes

Total:
2 hours

Yield:
Makes 16 buns

Jerry's Cinnamon Buns

There is nothing Jerry loves more than cinnamon buns. Nothing. So I came up with a substitute for the ones loaded with fat and calories that he'll sometimes eat on the road.

Photograph page 32.

SPONGE

- 1½ cups lukewarm nonfat (skim) milk
- ¼ cup 100% orange juice
- 2 (¼-ounce) packets active dry yeast
- ¼ cup granulated sugar

DOUGH

- 2 cups all-purpose flour
- 2 cups whole-wheat pastry flour
- ¼ cup nonfat (skim) milk powder
- ¾ teaspoon salt
- ½ cup **carrot puree**
- 1 large egg
- 3 tablespoons trans-fat-free soft tub margarine spread
- Nonstick cooking spray
- ½ cup firmly packed light or dark brown sugar
- 2 tablespoons ground cinnamon

GLAZE

- ¼ cup **cauliflower puree**
- 3 tablespoons confectioners' sugar
- 1 teaspoon pure vanilla extract
- 1 teaspoon 100% orange juice

1. To make the sponge, place the milk in a small glass bowl and microwave 40 to 50 seconds on high until the mixture is lukewarm. Stir in the orange juice, yeast, and sugar. Set aside in a warm place until foamy, about 10 to 15 minutes.

2. To make the dough, in the bowl of a standing mixer using a dough hook, combine both types of flour, the milk powder, and salt, and mix on low until combined. With the mixer still on low speed, add the yeast mixture, carrot puree, and egg. Increase the speed to medium and knead for 5 minutes.

3. Add the margarine and run the mixer 1 minute more—the dough will become sticky and will cling to the hook. With floured fingers, remove the dough stuck to the hook and place it in the bowl. Cover the bowl with plastic wrap and let the dough rise in a warm place until doubled, about 1 hour.

1 serving = 1 bun
Calories: 203, Carbohydrate: 39 g, Protein: 5 g, Total Fat: 3 g, Saturated Fat: 0.5 g, Sodium: 165 mg, Fiber: 3.5 g

4. After dough has doubled in size, place it on a cutting board with floured hands. Cut the dough in half.

5. Coat a large baking sheet with cooking spray and place half the dough on it. Flatten the dough out with your fingers, patting the edges to make them even. Sprinkle the surface of the dough with half of the brown sugar and 1 tablespoon of the cinnamon.

6. Roll the longest edge of the dough away from you to form a log. With a serrated knife, slice the dough into 1 inch rounds and flip them swirl-side down on the baking sheet.

7. Repeat steps 5 and 6 with the remaining dough.

8. Preheat the oven to 350°F while the rolls rise for 15 minutes more.

9. Meanwhile, make the glaze. Whisk all the ingredients for the glaze in a small bowl and set aside.

10. Bake the buns until they are cooked through but still soft to the touch, 18 to 20 minutes. Remove and cool before drizzling with the glaze.

Joy:
These cinnamon buns have about one-tenth the fat of the ones you buy at the mall, plus offer up a splash of vitamin C thanks to the cauliflower frosting.

Prep:
10 minutes

Total:
20 minutes

Yield:
Serves 4

Banana Chocolate-Chip Waffles

A brunch favorite. It takes just a few gooey, melted chocolate chips to make these waffles feel like a special treat on a weekend morning.

- 1 cup whole-wheat pastry flour
- 1 teaspoon baking soda
- ¼ teaspoon baking powder
- ¼ teaspoon salt
- 3 tablespoons canola oil
- 2 large egg whites
- ½ cup low-fat (1%) buttermilk
- ½ cup **carrot puree**
- 1 ripe banana, mashed (about ½ cup)
- 2 tablespoons bittersweet or dark chocolate chips
- Nonstick cooking spray

1. Preheat a waffle iron on high. In a large bowl or zipper-lock plastic bag, mix the flour, baking soda, baking powder, and salt. In another large bowl, beat the oil, egg whites, buttermilk, carrot puree, and banana with an electric mixer. Mix on low speed for 1 minute until smooth. Stir in the chocolate chips.

2. Add the flour mixture. Stir with a wooden spoon until just combined—the batter will be lumpy. Coat the waffle iron with cooking spray. Ladle ⅛ to ¼ cup of the batter into each compartment of the iron. Cook until the top of the iron releases easily and the waffle is lightly brown, 4 to 5 minutes. Serve immediately.

Jessica:
My rule—chocolate chips at breakfast only happen on weekends or holidays.

Calories: 298, Carbohydrate: 40 g, Protein: 7 g, Total Fat: 13.5 g, Saturated Fat: 2 g, Sodium: 565 mg, Fiber: 6.5 g

Prep:
10 minutes

Total:
25 minutes

Yield:
Serves 4

Scrambled Egg Muffins

We eat lots of eggs—specifically egg whites combined with a whole egg, to lighten things up. Here I've added chickpeas to keep things low in fat but high in protein.

- Nonstick cooking spray
- 4 slices nitrate-free turkey bacon
- 3 large egg whites
- 1 large egg
- ½ cup chopped, low-sodium chickpeas, rinsed and drained
- ¼ cup nonfat (skim) milk
- 4 teaspoons grated Parmesan

1. Preheat the oven to 400°F. Coat an 8-inch square piece of aluminum foil with cooking spray and lay the bacon on the foil. Transfer to the oven and bake for 10–15 minutes while you prepare the egg filling.

2. In a small bowl, whisk the egg whites, egg, chickpeas, and milk. In a 6-cup muffin tin, coat 4 of the cups with cooking spray. Divide the egg mixture among the 4 cups. Remove the bacon from the oven and snip with scissors or thinly slice. Sprinkle the bacon over the eggs and top with 1 teaspoon of the Parmesan.

3. Bake until the eggs puff and are cooked through, 12 to 15 minutes. Remove from the muffin pan and cool slightly before serving.

Jessica:
This cute breakfast can be taken on the run, yet is elegant enough for a sit-down brunch.

Calories: 117, Carbohydrate: 6 g, Protein: 14 g, Total Fat: 4 g, Saturated Fat: 1 g, Sodium: 370 mg, Fiber: 2 g

Prep:
10 minutes

Total:
30 minutes

Yield:
Serves 4

Bacon and Egg Cups

These are simple to make. My kids love to help craft the little tortilla cups before they go into the muffin tin.

- Nonstick cooking spray
- 4 fajita-size (6-inch) whole-wheat tortillas
- 1 large egg
- 3 large egg whites
- ½ cup **cauliflower puree**
- 2 slices nitrate-free turkey bacon, chopped
- 4 tablespoons shredded reduced-fat (2%) cheddar cheese
- Handful of chopped tomatoes and scallions (optional)

1. Preheat the oven to 350°F. In a 6-cup muffin tin, coat 4 of the cups with cooking spray. Hold up a tortilla and make 2 pleats, folding the tortilla into a cup. Press it down on the counter, so that you make the bottom flat and then fit it into one of the sprayed muffin cups. Repeat with the remaining tortillas.

2. In a small bowl, whisk the egg, egg whites, and cauliflower puree until smooth. Distribute the egg mixture among the four tortillas. Sprinkle with the bacon and cheddar cheese. Bake, uncovered, until the egg is cooked through and the cheese is melted and lightly browned, about 15 to 20 minutes. Serve topped with chopped tomatoes and scallions.

Julian:
I love how crispy the cup gets. It's like eating a chip in the morning!

Calories: 153, Carbohydrate: 14 g, Protein: 12.5 g, Total Fat: 5.5 g, Saturated Fat: 1.5 g, Sodium: 465 mg, Fiber: 0.5 g

Prep:
5 minutes

Total:
40 minutes

Yield:
Serves 6

Bird's Nest

Pasta that's crunchy AND cheesy is irresistible, especially for breakfast! This looks so pretty, no one will guess you used last night's leftover spaghetti.

- 2 cups leftover cooked whole-wheat spaghetti
- ½ cup **cauliflower puree**
- ¼ cup grated Parmesan
- 2 teaspoons cornstarch
- Pinch of salt
- ¼ cup flaxseed meal
- 1 tablespoon canola oil
- 6 large eggs

1. Combine the spaghetti, cauliflower puree, Parmesan, cornstarch, salt, and flaxseed meal in a medium bowl.

2. Set a large nonstick skillet over medium-high heat. Add ½ teaspoon of the canola oil. Take some of the pasta and form it into an O shape, leaving a 2½-inch opening in the center. Sauté 2 to 3 minutes until brown.

3. Carefully flip the O over. Crack 1 of the eggs into the center of the O, taking care not to break the yolk. Cover and cook 2 to 3 minutes longer, until the egg is cooked to your liking.

4. Repeat with the remaining pasta and eggs to make 6 nests. Sprinkle with salt just before serving. Serve warm!

Joy:
Eggs are a good source of choline, a vital nutrient that supports brain development in kids.

Calories: 205, Carbohydrate: 19 g, Protein: 12 g, Total Fat: 10 g, Saturated Fat: 2 g, Sodium: 175 mg, Fiber: 4.5 g

Whole Grains: The Smart Start

Uutritionists often say that breakfast is the most important meal of the day. Whole grains are an especially healthful choice for breakfast because they are packed with nutrients and fiber and leave you feeling satisfied. But for me, mornings are when I have the least time. So, here are some ways to get the great benefits of whole grains without a lot of fuss.

Hot Brown Rice Cereal: I try to cook extra brown rice at dinner (without salt) so I can use it for breakfast in the morning. Heat about 3 cups cooked brown rice with 1 tablespoon trans-fat-free soft tub margarine, and a sprinkling of raisins or sliced bananas. Serve with warmed low-fat milk or soy or rice milk, and a little bit of honey or brown sugar. I top with a handful of sliced, toasted almonds or walnuts (toast them on high in a sauté pan while heating up the rice).

Yogurt Smoothie: Use low-fat yogurt as a base and stir in raw, uncooked oats, ground flaxseed, or wheat germ. Add some fresh or frozen fruit for color and sweetness, or, if you have a bit of fresh mint, dice a leaf and sprinkle on top. Throw it all in a blender with some ice cubes and you have a delicious smoothie. No cooking required!

Homemade Muesli: I love to make my own muesli. I usually have everything in my cupboard so I can throw it together within minutes. In a bowl or plastic bag, add lots of whole oats (not the instant kind) as the base. Then add some whole-wheat flakes and/or bran cereal. I add brown rice crispies to make it more appealing to my kids. Chop up some dates, add dried raisins or cranberries (the kind sweetened with fruit juice only—no sugars!), flaxseed, and some chopped walnuts. Shredded coconut is nice, if you have it. Mix in Greek yogurt and let it sit for a while. Finally, drizzle with honey before eating.

Mealtime

Chicken and Rice Soup

My family cannot get enough of this rich and creamy soup. My kids would prefer to eat this above anything else. I add a squeeze of lemon at the end—my friend's Italian grandmother taught me this old Mediterranean secret.

Prep:
30 minutes

Total:
55 minutes

Yield:
Serves 8

- 2 carrots, peeled
- 1 stalk celery
- 1 small onion, peeled
- 2 tablespoons olive oil
- ¼ teaspoon pepper
- ½ teaspoon sweet paprika
- ¼ cup short-grain white rice
- 1 quart water
- 1 quart low fat, reduced-sodium chicken broth
- 2 skinless chicken breasts on the bone
- 1 cup **cauliflower puree**
- ½ cup **carrot puree**
- 1 tablespoon cornstarch
- 2 tablespoons reduced-fat cream cheese, at room temperature
- ¼ cup freshly squeezed lemon juice

1. Finely chop the carrots, celery, and onion by hand or in a food processor. Heat the olive oil a large stockpot over medium-high heat. Add the chopped vegetables, pepper, and paprika. Cook until the vegetables soften but do not brown, 6 to 8 minutes. Add the rice and cook 1 to 2 minutes more, until the ends of the rice turn translucent.

2. Add the water and broth and bring to a boil. Add the chicken and cover. Turn off the heat and let the chicken cook in the hot water until it's no longer pink at the bone, 25 to 30 minutes. Once the chicken has cooked through, remove the meat from the bone, shred it, and return it to the pot.

3. Stir the purees into the soup. In a small bowl, mash the cornstarch into the cream cheese. Remove 1 cup of the soup and whisk it into the cream cheese mixture until it is smooth and all lumps are gone. Stir the soup and cream-cheese mixture back into the pot and warm through if necessary. Stir in the lemon juice just before serving.

Julian:
I could eat this every day.

Calories: 114, Carbohydrate: 10 g, Protein: 10 g, Total Fat: 4 g, Saturated Fat: 1 g, Sodium: 240 mg, Fiber: 1.5 g

Tomato Soup

I love Tomato Soup with grilled cheese. My children, predictably, won't touch tomato soup. But when I add some mini turkey meatballs, they'll eat "meatball" soup with no problem.

Shown here with Protein-Packed Grilled Cheese (recipe page 50).

Prep:
15 minutes

Total:
30 minutes

Yield:
Serves 8

- 2 tablespoons olive oil
- 2 stalks celery, chopped
- 1 small onion, minced
- 3 cloves garlic, minced
- 1 (28-ounce) can "no salt added" whole, peeled tomatoes
- 1 cup **sweet potato puree**
- ½ cup **broccoli puree**
- 1 quart (4 cups) low-fat, reduced-sodium beef broth
- 1 bay leaf
- ¼ teaspoon pepper
- 4 ounces reduced-fat cream cheese, at room temperature

1. Warm the oil in a large stockpot over medium-high heat. Add the celery, onion, and garlic. Cook until the onion softens, 6 to 8 minutes. Add the tomatoes, sweet potato and broccoli purees, broth, bay leaf, and pepper.

2. Bring to a boil. Reduce to a slow simmer and cook until the soup begins to thicken, about 10 minutes. Off the heat, add the cream cheese. Remove the bay leaf. Blend with an immersion or stick blender until smooth. Serve immediately.

Joy:

This soup hits the antioxidant trifecta. Tomatoes provide lycopene and vitamin C, and sweet potato is an excellent source of beta-carotene.

Calories: 130, Carbohydrate: 15 g, Protein: 4.5 g, Total Fat: 6.5 g, Saturated Fat: 2 g, Sodium: 285 mg, Fiber: 3.5 g

Prep:
10 minutes

Total:
15 minutes

Yield:
Serves 4

Protein-Packed Grilled Cheese

The bean spread under the melted cheese makes this a really satisfying meal. I have also served these as little appetizers, especially when my vegetarian friends come for dinner.

Photograph page 48.

BEAN SPREAD

- 1 cup low-sodium white beans, such as navy or cannellini, drained and rinsed
- 2 teaspoons lemon juice
- ¼ cup part-skim ricotta
- 1 teaspoon olive oil
- ½ clove garlic, roughly chopped
- ¼ teaspoon salt
- ⅛ teaspoon pepper

- 4 slices whole-wheat bread
- 8 tablespoons bean spread
- 8 tablespoons shredded part-skim mozzarella

1. For the bean spread, place the beans, lemon juice, ricotta, olive oil, garlic, salt, and pepper in a mini-chopper and blend until smooth. Spread each slice of bread with 2 tablespoonfuls of the bean spread. Divide the cheese among the 4 slices and toast in a toaster oven until the cheese is golden and melted.

2. Store remaining dip in an airtight container. Can be refrigerated for up to 1 week.

Joy:
Beans are an excellent source of fiber (about 6 grams per half cup), something that most people could use more of in their diet.

Calories: 157, Carbohydrate: 20 g, Protein: 10 g, Total Fat: 4.5 g, Saturated Fat: 2 g, Sodium: 370 mg, Fiber: 4 g

Other Mothers Know Best!

"Necessity, who is the mother of invention..."

That's what Plato wrote more than 2,000 years ago—and it's still true. But honestly, who deals with necessity more than mothers? When I polled my friends for their favorite ways of helping their families eat better, I was amazed at how creative and skillful their ideas were. I learned a lot, so just as before, I've decided to sprinkle their wisdom throughout this book. Because really, isn't motherhood the mother of invention?

Nanette, mother of Henry (8) and Lily (10):

Whole-wheat waffles are a great source of vitamins and fiber, but my kids get bored with them. For Henry, my snowboarder, I top the waffle with a "mountain" of vanilla yogurt onto which he sprinkles a "blizzard" of coconut snow. Lily, my artist, swirls peanut butter and strawberry jam on her waffle for an inspired and delicious masterpiece!

Butternut Tomato Soup

This nondairy, sweet, and tangy soup works for everyone.
I often turn it into a complete meal by dicing up chicken and
serving some pasta on the side (which my kids quickly dump
into the soup).

Prep:
25 minutes

Total:
1 hour

Yield:
Serves 10

- 3 shallots, peeled
- 4 stalks celery
- 2 tablespoons olive oil
- 5 cups diced, peeled, and seeded butternut squash (1 small squash, about 2½ pounds)
- 1½ quarts low-fat, reduced-sodium vegetable broth
- 1 (15-ounce) can diced tomatoes, preferably "no salt added"
- ½ teaspoon salt
- ½ teaspoon pepper

TOPPING (OPTIONAL)
- 1 cup silken tofu
- 2 tablespoons grated Parmesan
- ¼ teaspoon salt

1. Slice the shallots and celery with the slicing attachment on a food processor. Heat the oil in a large stockpot over medium-high heat. Add the shallots and celery. Cook until the shallots begin to soften but not brown, 5 to 7 minutes.

2. Add the butternut squash, vegetable broth, diced tomatoes, salt, and pepper. Bring to a boil, then reduce to a simmer.

3. Cover and cook until the butternut squash becomes tender and is easily mashed with the back of a metal spoon, about 45 minutes.

4. Puree the soup with an immersion blender, or in a standing blender or food processor in batches.

5. To make the topping, place the tofu, Parmesan, and salt in a mini-chopper or food processor. Whip until smooth and serve with the soup.

Jessica:
When I let my kids decide what to add to this healthy soup, it becomes fun and resistance-free!

Calories: 91, Carbohydrate: 12 g, Protein: 4 g, Total Fat: 3.5 g, Saturated Fat: 0.5 g, Sodium: 260 mg, Fiber: 2.5 g

My Everyday Healthy Shortcuts

We're all looking for simple ways to eat better, right? Sometimes it's just a matter of making a few small changes to the way we cook, because, in the end, every little bit adds up.

- To minimize added fat, use an oil-based cooking spray when searing meats or sautéing vegetables instead of pouring in oil from a bottle. I try to use my cast-iron skillet as much as possible: It cooks food evenly with very little oil and as an added bonus is a good way to add a little iron to our diet!

- Replace some whole eggs with egg whites for a lighter breakfast.

- Cut the fat in meatloaf, meatballs, or meat sauces by replacing ground beef with ground turkey or ground chicken breast. Add a little grated yellow squash, carrot, or zucchini or some veggie puree to keep the mixture moist.

- Replace whole egg or milk with egg whites or 1% buttermilk when coating chicken or fish in breadcrumbs. Mix some flaxseed meal into the coating for added goodness.

- Cut down on added salt in salad dressings, soups, and stews. Get in the habit of using other flavorings, like fresh herbs or lemon, lime, or orange zest.

Honey Mustard Chicken

If you love pretzels and honey mustard you will love this! The crushed pretzels add an extra crunch that's often missing from regular breadcrumb coatings.

Prep:
20 minutes

Total:
30 minutes

Yield:
Serves 4

- 1 cup whole-wheat breadcrumbs
- ½ cup finely crushed unsalted pretzels
- 1 tablespoon grated Parmesan
- ½ teaspoon sweet paprika
- ½ teaspoon garlic powder
- ½ teaspoon onion powder
- 1 cup **sweet potato puree**
- 3 tablespoons honey
- 1 large egg
- 1 teaspoon Dijon mustard
- 1½ pounds boneless, skinless chicken breasts, cut into small chunks
- Nonfat cooking spray
- 1 tablespoon olive oil

1. On a piece of waxed paper or aluminum foil, stir breadcrumbs, pretzel crumbs, Parmesan, paprika, garlic powder, and onion powder together.

2. In a shallow dish, mix the sweet potato puree, honey, egg, and mustard. Dip the chicken chunks into the sweet potato mixture and then coat in the breadcrumb mixture. Set aside.

3. Coat a large skillet with cooking spray, add the olive oil, and set over medium-high heat. Brown the chicken on the first side, cooking 4 to 5 minutes, until the breadcrumb coating is crispy and golden. Turn the chicken and cook 4 to 5 minutes more, until the chicken is cooked through. Serve immediately (or cool completely before packing in an airtight container).

Sascha:
I love pretzels! I help make this meal by being the pretzel crusher.

Calories: 522, Carbohydrate: 64 g, Protein: 48 g, Total Fat: 8 g, Saturated Fat: 1.5 g, Sodium: 440 mg, Fiber: 6.5 g

Prep:
15 minutes

Total:
25 minutes

Yield:
Serves 6

Lemon Chicken

Hands down, this is my favorite chicken dish in the world. It is juicy and rich-tasting, yet light and lemony. What a combination! Shown here with Cauliflower Gratin (recipe page 114).

- 1 tablespoon chopped garlic
- 2 tablespoons plus 1 teaspoon olive oil, separated
- 3 cups low-fat, reduced-sodium chicken broth
- 2 tablespoons freshly squeezed lemon juice
- 2 teaspoons water
- 2 teaspoons cornstarch
- ½ cup **cauliflower puree**
- 1 tablespoon chopped parsley (optional)
- 2 large egg whites
- 1 large egg
- 1 cup whole-wheat flour
- ½ teaspoon salt
- 1 teaspoon garlic powder
- 6 boneless, skinless chicken breast cutlets (about 2¼ pounds)

1. In a heavy-bottomed saucepan over medium heat, sauté the chopped garlic in 1 teaspoon of the olive oil until it begins to turn golden brown. Add the chicken broth, turn the heat to high, and reduce by half, about 8 minutes. Add the lemon juice.

2. In a small bowl, combine the water and cornstarch. Slowly stir the cornstarch mixture into the boiling chicken broth. The mixture will thicken quickly. Add the cauliflower puree. Sprinkle in parsley, if desired. Cover to keep warm and set aside.

3. Meanwhile, begin heating the remaining 2 tablespoons olive oil in a large heavy-bottomed skillet over medium heat. Whisk the egg whites and egg in a shallow bowl. Combine the flour, salt, and garlic powder on a large plate. Dredge each chicken cutlet in the seasoned flour and then dip in the egg mixture. Drop the cutlets directly into the heated skillet. Sauté 4 to 5 minutes per side, until the chicken is golden brown and cooked through. Add the lemon sauce and cook 2 to 3 minutes more to combine flavors. Serve.

Calories: 333, Carbohydrate: 18 g, Protein: 45 g, Total Fat: 8.5 g, Saturated Fat: 1.5 g, Sodium: 565 mg, Fiber: 3 g

Chicken and Biscuits

This is a more nutritious and lower-fat take on a traditional favorite, without sacrificing flavor. It's also a quick meal to prepare. Light, fluffy biscuits top the rich gravy—this is comfort food for everyone.

Prep:
30 minutes

Total:
1 hour

Yield:
Serves 6

- 1 tablespoon olive oil
- 2 boneless, skinless chicken breasts, cubed (about 1 pound)
- ⅛ teaspoon freshly ground black pepper
- 1 (8.5-ounce) can reduced-fat cream of celery soup
- ½ cup nonfat (skim) milk
- ½ cup **pumpkin**, **carrot**, or **sweet potato puree**

BISCUIT TOPPING
- 1½ cups whole-wheat flour
  2 teaspoons baking powder
- ¼ teaspoon salt
- ½ cup trans-fat-free, soft tub margarine spread
- 1 large egg, beaten
- ¼ cup honey
- ½ teaspoon cream of tartar
- ¾ cup low-fat (1%) buttermilk

1. Heat the oil in a flameproof casserole or Dutch oven over high heat. Sprinkle the chicken with pepper. Add it to the casserole and cook until the chicken begins to brown, 4 to 5 minutes. Stir in the soup, milk, and vegetable puree until all ingredients are well combined. Remove from heat.

2. Preheat the oven to 375°F. Prepare the biscuits. In a large bowl, combine the flour, baking powder, and salt. Rub the margarine into the flour with your fingertips until the mixture resembles coarse crumbs. Add the egg, honey, cream of tartar, and buttermilk all at once. Mix just until a soft dough forms. Dot the biscuit dough over the chicken mixture. Bake 20 to 25 minutes, uncovered, until the biscuits are cooked through and golden on top. Serve immediately.

With pumpkin puree:
Calories: 442,
Carbohydrate: 41 g, Protein: 25 g,
Total Fat: 21 g, Saturated Fat: 3.5 g,
Sodium: 745 mg, Fiber: 5 g

With carrot puree:
Calories: 447,
Carbohydrate: 42 g, Protein: 25 g,
Total Fat: 21 g, Saturated Fat: 3.5 g,
Sodium: 765 mg, Fiber: 5 g

With sweet potato puree:
Calories: 455,
Carbohydrate: 43 g, Protein: 25 g,
Total Fat: 21 g, Saturated Fat: 3.5 g,
Sodium: 755 mg, Fiber: 5 g

Prep:
30 minutes

Total:
50 minutes

Yield:
Serves 6

Chicken Satay

Anything served on a stick is exciting to my family. This sauce is sensational—"peanutty" and sweet. Serve with veggies and rice for a fun dinner.

SAUCE

- 1 clove garlic, cut in half
- ¼ cup lite coconut milk
- ¼ cup **sweet potato puree**
- 3 tablespoons natural peanut butter (creamy)
- 2 tablespoons reduced-sodium soy sauce
- 2 tablespoons lime juice (about 1 large lime)
- Pinch of cayenne pepper (optional)

SKEWERS

- 1½ pounds boneless, skinless chicken breasts
- 30 (10-inch) wooden skewers
- ½ teaspoon salt
- ½ teaspoon garlic powder
- ¼ teaspoon pepper
- ¼ teaspoon sweet paprika
- 2 tablespoons olive oil

1. Chop the garlic in a mini-chopper. Add the coconut milk, sweet potato puree, peanut butter, soy sauce, lime juice, and cayenne. Blend until smooth. Set aside.

2. Cut the chicken into thin strips, about 1-inch wide. Thread the chicken onto the skewers. Sprinkle with the salt, garlic powder, pepper, and paprika.

3. Warm 1 tablespoon of the olive oil in a large skillet. Add half the skewers. Cook 7 to 8 minutes per side, turning once, until the chicken is cooked through and no longer pink. Transfer to a platter and add the remaining tablespoon of oil. Repeat with the rest of the skewers. Serve immediately with dipping sauce.

Calories: 242, Carbohydrate: 6 g, Protein: 29 g, Total Fat: 10.5 g, Saturated Fat: 2 g, Sodium: 475 mg, Fiber: 1 g

Prep:
30 minutes

Total:
1 hour 10 minutes

Yield:
Serves 6

Chicken Enchiladas

This is a great dish for a potluck dinner because all the work can be done in advance—it just needs to be popped in the oven. I made these for our kids' class dinner, and the parents demolished the platters.

- Nonstick cooking spray
- 1 tablespoon olive oil
- 2 boneless, skinless chicken breasts, cubed (about ¾ pound)
- ½ teaspoon garlic powder
- ¼ teaspoon pepper
- ½ cup **sweet potato** or **carrot puree**
- ¼ cup fat-free sour cream
- 1 cup shredded, reduced-fat (2%) cheddar cheese or part-skim mozzarella, divided
- 6 (9-inch) whole-grain or whole-wheat flour tortillas
- ½ cup **spinach puree**
- ½ cup mild tomato salsa

1. Preheat the oven to 350°F. Coat a 9 x 12-inch baking dish with cooking spray. Warm the oil in a large skillet over medium-high heat. Sprinkle the chicken with garlic powder and pepper. Cook the chicken 4 to 5 minutes, stirring occasionally, until it is cooked through and no longer pink in the center. Off the heat, mix the sweet potato or carrot puree, sour cream, and half the cheese into the skillet.

2. Fill each tortilla with the chicken mixture and roll up. Place seam-side down in the prepared baking dish. Dot the tops of the enchiladas with spinach puree. Spoon the salsa over the enchiladas and sprinkle with the remaining cheese. Cover the dish with aluminum foil and bake until the cheese melts and the filling is hot, 35 to 40 minutes.

With sweet potato puree:
Calories: 310, Carbohydrate: 39 g, Protein: 24 g,
Total Fat: 11 g, Saturated Fat: 3 g,
Sodium: 755 mg, Fiber: 11 g

With carrot puree:
Calories: 302, Carbohydrate: 37 g, Protein: 25 g,
Total Fat: 11 g, Saturated Fat: 3 g,
Sodium: 760 mg, Fiber: 11 g

Prep:
25 minutes

Total:
45 minutes

Yield:
Serves 4

Chicken Parmesan

I have been making Chicken Parmesan since I was in high school. It was my first specialty in the kitchen. The recent addition of spinach puree adds crispiness and juiciness— I wish I had known about it long ago!

- 1½ cups jarred marinara sauce
- ½ cup **carrot puree**
- 4 boneless, skinless chicken breasts (about 1½ pounds)
- Juice from 1 lemon
- 2 large egg whites
- ½ cup **spinach puree**
- ¼ teaspoon pepper
- ½ cup whole-wheat flour
- ¾ cup whole-wheat breadcrumbs
- Nonstick cooking spray
- 1 tablespoon olive oil
- ½ cup grated part-skim mozzarella
- 2 tablespoons grated Parmesan

Joy:

Hard to fathom, but one portion of fried chicken parm can ooze with over 50g of fat! Jessica's baked version, with 10g of fat, is a refreshing alternative, plus it's loaded with lean protein and calcium-rich cheese.

1. Preheat the oven to 400°F. In a small bowl, mix the marinara sauce and carrot puree. Pour 1 cup of the marinara–carrot mixture into an 8 x 12-inch dish. Set aside.

2. Place the chicken between 2 sheets of waxed paper. With a mallet, pound the chicken thin. Place in a colander and rinse under cold water. Squeeze the lemon juice on top of the chicken and let it drain.

3. In a bowl, whisk the egg whites and spinach puree. Sprinkle the chicken with pepper. Place the flour on a sheet of waxed paper. Place the breadcrumbs in a shallow dish. Dredge the chicken in the flour, dip in the egg wash, then press into the breadcrumbs to coat both sides.

4. Coat 2 medium-sized skillets with cooking spray. Divide the oil between the 2 skillets and heat over medium-high. When the oil is hot, add the chicken and cook 5 to 6 minutes, turning once, until both sides are brown. Transfer to the prepared dish and lay over the sauce. Top with the remaining sauce, then sprinkle with the cheeses.

5. Bake in the preheated oven 15 to 20 minutes uncovered, until the cheese is melted. Serve immediately.

Calories: 490, Carbohydrate: 46 g, Protein: 54 g, Total Fat: 10.5 g, Saturated Fat: 3 g, Sodium: 765 mg, Fiber: 8.5 g

Other Mothers Know Best!

We all know how hard it is to shop with kids—it takes me twice as long and costs twice as much! To quiet them, and get done and out of the store, I end up buying things I don't want and don't need. Ideally, we'd shop alone, but since this is not an ideal world, I've developed my own strategies and picked up some ideas from my friends. In general, I try to stick to the perimeter aisles where fruits and veggies, dairy, meat, and fish are located. I avoid the center aisles, where the processed foods and sweetened beverages are, or leave them until last.

Liz, mother of Lucy (4) and Danielle (6):

I try to get my two kids involved. So there are fewer disagreements in the store, we create a list in advance. Then I try to make the shopping experience fun by turning it into a scavenger hunt. I have the kids ask the store employees where things are located.

Kate, mother of Dylan (3):

I carry a book in my bag, a bottle of water, small toys—anything to keep her occupied or from reaching for candy at the checkout!

Martha, mother of Jaden (8):

As a single mom, I need my son's help with lots of things around the house. One of his jobs is to be in charge of our shopping list—at home he practices his writing by making a list of things we need. Then, in the store, he's in charge of checking off the items as we find them. I always try to go shopping when the store is empty and quiet, so we can come and go quickly.

Teriyaki Chicken

A family favorite served weekly at our house, with a side of rice and broccoli. Shown here with Rice Pilaf (recipe page 113).

Prep:
30 minutes

Total:
55 minutes

Yield:
Serves 4

TERIYAKI SAUCE

- 3 tablespoons reduced-sodium soy sauce
- ¼ cup **carrot puree**
- 1 tablespoon firmly packed dark brown sugar
- ¼ cup 100% orange juice
- 1 clove garlic, cut in half
- 2 green onions, cut in thirds
- ½-inch piece fresh ginger, sliced (no need to peel)

- 1 tablespoon olive oil
- 4 boneless, skinless chicken breasts (about 1½ pounds)
- ¼ teaspoon pepper
- ¼ teaspoon sweet paprika

1. Preheat the oven to 350°F. Place all the ingredients for the teriyaki sauce in a small saucepan. Bring to a boil. Reduce to a simmer, then cook until the mixture thickens, 8 to 10 minutes. Remove the garlic, onions, and ginger.

2. Heat the olive oil in a large ovenproof skillet over high heat. Sprinkle the chicken with the pepper and paprika. When the oil is hot, add the chicken and cook 4 to 5 minutes per side, until both sides are golden. Off the heat, carefully pour in the teriyaki sauce. Slide the skillet into the oven. Bake until the chicken is cooked through, 20 to 25 minutes. Serve immediately.

Shepherd:
This chicken tastes sweet!

Sascha:
Mom also makes us teriyaki salmon using the same sauce.

Calories: 253, Carbohydrate: 8 g, Protein: 41 g, Total Fat: 5.5 g, Saturated Fat: 1 g, Sodium: 555 mg, Fiber: 1 g

Prep:
20 minutes

Total:
30 minutes

Yield:
Makes 2 medium
pizzas. Serves 8

Chicken Pizza

Fresh and crispy from the oven, homemade pizza is irresistible. To make it more fun (and nutritious), serve with a mix of toppings—peppers, fresh basil, mushrooms.

- Nonstick cooking spray
- 2 boneless, skinless chicken breasts (about ¾ pound)
- ½ teaspoon garlic powder
- ¼ teaspoon sweet paprika
- ¼ teaspoon pepper
- 2 teaspoons olive oil
- 1½ cups jarred marinara sauce
- ½ cup **carrot puree**
- 1 pound frozen pizza dough, preferably whole-wheat or whole-grain, thawed
- 2 cups grated part-skim mozzarella

1. Preheat the oven to 450°F. Coat 2 large baking sheets with cooking spray. Sprinkle the chicken with the garlic powder, paprika, and pepper. Heat the oil in a large ovenproof skillet over medium-high heat. Brown the chicken on both sides 5 to 7 minutes, turning once, until it is cooked through and no longer pink in the center. When the chicken is cool to the touch, thinly slice.

2. In a medium bowl, mix the marinara sauce and carrot puree until smooth. Cut the dough in half. Roll out each piece of dough on a lightly floured surface and shape into a round disk with your fingers.

3. Place the dough onto the prepared baking sheets. Top each pizza with the sauce. Top with the sliced chicken, then sprinkle with the cheese. Bake until the crust is cooked and the cheese is lightly browned, 10 to 15 minutes. Allow to cool 5 minutes before slicing.

Sascha:

Pizza is our favorite food. We love it when Mommy makes it nice and cheesy!

Calories: 297, Carbohydrate: 31 g, Protein: 24 g, Total Fat: 9 g, Saturated Fat: 3.5 g, Sodium: 650 mg, Fiber: 3.5 g

Balsamic Chicken Sandwich

This is based on a sandwich Jerry and I fell in love with in Italy. For a healthier version, substitute the Italian bread with whole-grain rolls or whole-wheat bread. It is delicious any way you serve it!

Prep:
30 minutes

Total:
40 minutes

Yield:
Serves 6

- 2 pounds boneless, skinless chicken breasts, cubed
- ½ teaspoon salt
- ½ teaspoon pepper
- ¼ cup whole-wheat flour
- 3 tablespoons olive oil
- 3 cloves garlic, minced
- 1 cup low-fat, reduced-sodium chicken broth
- ½ cup balsamic vinegar
- 6 tablespoons firmly packed dark brown sugar
- ½ cup **broccoli puree**
- 6 large slices tomato
- 6 ciabatta rolls, or 6 large slices crusty Italian bread
- ½ cup grated part-skim mozzarella

1. Sprinkle the chicken with salt and pepper. Place the flour on a sheet of waxed paper. Toss the chicken chunks in the flour and coat completely. Preheat the oven to 350°F.

2. Warm the oil in a large skillet over medium-high heat. Add the chicken and garlic. Decrease the heat to medium and continue to cook until the chicken begins to brown and the garlic becomes fragrant, 8 to 10 minutes.

3. Add the chicken broth, vinegar, and brown sugar. Bring to a boil. Cover and simmer 10 to 15 minutes, until the chicken is cooked through and no longer pink in the center. Add the puree and cook 2 to 3 minutes more, until the flavors are well blended.

4. Place the bread on a large baking sheet. Top each with a tomato slice. Divide the chicken between the 6 pieces of bread and top with mozzarella. Bake until the cheese is melted and edges of the bread are crisp, 5 to 7 minutes. Serve immediately.

Jerry:
I love when Jessica does her own take on restaurant meals. This one makes me feel like we're back in Italy.

Calories: 416, Carbohydrate: 34 g, Protein: 42 g, Total Fat: 11 g, Saturated Fat: 2.5 g, Sodium: 615 mg, Fiber: 3 g

Prep:
10 minutes

Total:
15 minutes

Yield:
Serves 4

Creamy Chicken

Every child who eats at my house has at least two helpings of this. They are passionate about it! Serve with pasta or rice.

- 1 pound boneless, skinless chicken breast
- ¼ teaspoon salt
- 1½ teaspoons garlic powder
- 2 tablespoons trans-fat-free soft tub margarine spread
- 1½ tablespoons whole-wheat flour
- 1 cup low-fat, reduced-sodium chicken broth
- 1 cup nonfat (skim) milk
- 1 cup **cauliflower** or **butternut squash puree**

1. Wash the chicken and cut into small, 1-inch pieces. Place in a zipper-lock plastic bag. Pour in the salt and garlic powder. Close the bag, then shake and squeeze the bag to spread the spices around.

2. Heat 1 tablespoon of the margarine in a large heavy-bottomed skillet. Add the chicken and lightly brown it, about 2 to 3 minutes. Take the chicken out with a slotted spoon and set aside.

3. Add the remaining tablespoon of margarine to the skillet, then add the flour. Whisk in the chicken broth and stir for approximately 2 minutes, making sure that there are no lumps. When smooth, slowly add the milk.

4. Let mixture cook for 2 minutes, stirring occasionally as it thickens. Then add the chicken back to the pan until it is cooked through, about 4 minutes.

5. Add the puree. Then let the chicken sit off the heat, allowing the sauce to thicken.

With cauliflower puree:
Calories: 222, Carbohydrate: 8 g,
Protein: 30 g, Total Fat: 7 g, Saturated Fat: 1 g,
Sodium: 445 mg, Fiber: 1.5 g

With butternut squash puree:
Calories: 247, Carbohydrate: 15 g,
Protein: 30 g, Total Fat: 7 g, Saturated Fat: 1 g,
Sodium: 435 mg, Fiber: 3.5 g

Turkey Meatloaf

Lots of added vegetables here but no "green stuff" makes this a great option for very picky eaters. The flavor is amazing.

QUICK!

Prep:
5 minutes

Total:
55 minutes

Yield:
Serves 8

- Nonstick cooking spray
- 2 pounds lean ground turkey
- 1 teaspoon garlic powder
- 1 teaspoon onion powder
- 1 teaspoon salt
- ⅓ cup whole-wheat breadcrumbs
- 1 tablespoon Worcestershire sauce
- 3 large egg whites
- ½ cup **carrot puree**
- ½ cup **cauliflower puree**
- Jarred tomato sauce (optional)

1. Preheat the oven to 375°F. Coat a 9 x 5-inch loaf pan with cooking spray. Mix all the ingredients in a large bowl and stir to combine.

2. Press the mixture into the loaf pan. Bake until golden brown and no longer pink in the center, 50 to 55 minutes. Cut into slices and serve.

3. Serve with tomato sauce, if you wish.

Jessica:
This recipe gets you out of the kitchen in minutes—leaving time for other chores or activities.

Joy:
Using ground turkey (at least 90% lean) in place of fatty ground beef cuts way back on the saturated fat in this meatloaf. Trust me, your kids will not taste the difference.

Calories: 213, **Carbohydrate:** 8 g, **Protein:** 26 g, **Total Fat:** 8 g, **Saturated Fat:** 2 g, **Sodium:** 465 mg, **Fiber:** 1.5 g

Prep:
35 minutes

Total:
35 minutes

Yield:
Serves 4

Sweet and Sour Meatballs

This is not just cocktail party food—kids love eating these tasty mini meatballs with toothpicks as a fun meal served with egg noodles and veggies.

- 2 tablespoons olive oil
- 1 small onion, finely chopped
- 2 cloves garlic, minced
- 2 slices soft whole-wheat bread, crust removed, torn in pieces
- ½ cup nonfat plain yogurt
- ½ cup **broccoli puree**
- 1 large egg
- ½ pound ground chicken or turkey (at least 90% lean)
- ½ teaspoon salt
- ½ teaspoon nutmeg
- ¼ teaspoon pepper

SAUCE
- 2 teaspoons olive oil
- 1 medium onion, chopped
- 2 teaspoons firmly packed dark brown sugar
- ½ cup low-fat, reduced-sodium beef broth
- 1 tablespoon ketchup
- 2 teaspoons steak sauce
- ¼ cup crushed pineapple in natural juice, or ¼ cup fresh pureed pineapple
- 1 tablespoon orange marmalade

1. Preheat the oven to 350°F. Heat 1 tablespoon of the olive oil in a large skillet over medium heat. Add the onion and cook 7 to 8 minutes, stirring often, until the onion softens. Add the garlic and cook 1 minute more, until the garlic is fragrant. Place the bread in a large mixing bowl with the cooked onion and garlic, yogurt, broccoli puree, egg, chicken, salt, nutmeg, and pepper. Beat with an electric mixer on medium speed until smooth. Form into ½-inch meatballs and set on a sheet of waxed paper.

2. Heat the remaining olive oil in the skillet over medium-high heat. Add half of the meatballs and cook 7 to 8 minutes, turning occasionally, until they are browned. Transfer to a plate and repeat with the remaining meatballs.

3. Meanwhile, prepare the sauce. Heat the oil in a small saucepan. Add the onion and sugar. Cook 7 to 8 minutes, stirring occasionally, until the onions are soft and slightly browned. Add the remaining ingredients and bring to a boil, cooking 1 minute more. Puree with an immersion blender or transfer to a food processor and blend until smooth. Pour over the meatballs and serve.

Calories: 322, Carbohydrate: 19 g, Protein: 19 g, Total Fat: 15 g, Saturated Fat: 2.5 g, Sodium: 605 mg, Fiber: 4 g

Meatball Subs

Prep:
30 minutes

Total:
1 hour

Yield:
Serves 8

My kids love almost anything served in a bun. And Jerry says food that's wrapped in "fancy paper" always tastes delicious, no matter what it is. I send him to NY Mets games with this healthy, high-protein take on a regular sub.

- ½ cup whole-wheat breadcrumbs
- 1 cup low-fat, reduced-sodium chicken broth
- 1 cup **sweet potato puree**
- 1 large egg white
- 1 clove garlic, chopped
- ¼ teaspoon salt
- ¼ teaspoon pepper
- ½ pound ground beef (at least 90% lean)
- ½ pound ground turkey (all white meat)
- 1 tablespoon olive oil
- ½ onion, chopped
- 2 tablespoons tomato paste
- 1 (28-ounce) can "no salt added" diced tomatoes
- 8 whole-wheat hot dog rolls, warmed
- 1 cup grated part-skim mozzarella

1. In a large bowl, mix the breadcrumbs, ½ cup of the chicken broth, the puree, egg white, garlic, salt, and the pepper. Gently mix in the meat. Form meatballs, 2 inches in diameter, and place them on a sheet of waxed paper.

2. Heat the oil in a large stockpot over medium-high heat. Add the onions. Cook until they begin to soften, 4 to 6 minutes. Add the meatballs and continue to cook 8 to 10 minutes, turning the meatballs occasionally. Clear a small space in the pan and add the tomato paste. Cook 1 additional minute more, until the paste browns slightly. Then mix in the diced tomatoes and remaining broth.

3. Bring to a slow boil, then immediately reduce to a simmer. Cover and cook 35 to 40 minutes, occasionally stirring gently, until the meatballs are cooked through. Transfer 3 meatballs to each hot dog roll. Top each with 2 tablespoons of the sauce and sprinkle with cheese.

Calories: 311, Carbohydrate: 40 g, Protein: 19 g, Total Fat: 7.5 g, Saturated Fat: 2 g, Sodium: 590 mg, Fiber: 7 g

Prep:
20 minutes

Total:
20 minutes

Yield:
Serves 4

Orange Beef

This a leaner version of a favorite Chinese dish. Sometimes I'll make it extra spicy for Jerry or substitute tofu for our vegetarian friends.

- 1½ pounds filet or lean beef, cut into cubes, or 1 (14-ounce) package of firm tofu, drained and cut into ½-inch cubes
- ¼ cup cornstarch, plus 1 teaspoon
- ½ teaspoon pepper
- 2 tablespoons canola oil
- 2 tablespoons reduced-sodium soy sauce
- ½ cup 100% orange juice
- Zest of 1 orange
- ¼ cup warm water
- ½ cup **sweet potato puree**
- 1 tablespoon light brown sugar
- 1 teaspoon freshly grated ginger
- 1 teaspoon hot chili paste (if you are not using chili paste, add 2 cloves garlic)
- 2 medium carrots, sliced (about 1½ cups)
- 2 cups broccoli florets
- 1 tablespoon canola oil
- ¼ cup chopped scallions (optional)

1. Coat the beef or tofu with ¼ cup of the cornstarch and the pepper in a large bowl. Heat the 2 tablespoons of canola oil on high heat in a wok or sauté pan and then carefully add the cubed beef or tofu. Cook until golden brown and crispy, about 7 to 8 minutes, stirring once or twice. Transfer to paper towels to drain excess fat.

2. In a separate bowl, combine the soy sauce, orange juice, zest, water, sweet potato puree, brown sugar, ginger, chili paste or garlic, and the remaining cornstarch and mix until smooth.

3. In a clean sauté pan, sauté the carrots and broccoli in 1 tablespoon of oil for 1 to 2 minutes. Push the carrots off to the side, add the soy sauce mixture, and bring the sauce to a boil. Then add the beef or tofu to the pan and coat with the sauce. Cook 1 to 2 minutes more, until the sauce thickens. Garnish with scallions and serve immediately.

With beef:
Calories: 457, Carbohydrate: 28 g, Protein: 39 g, Total Fat: 20 g, Saturated Fat: 4 g, Sodium: 445 mg, Fiber: 3.5 g

With tofu:
Calories: 303, Carbohydrate: 31 g, Protein: 12 g, Total Fat: 14 g, Saturated Fat: 1 g, Sodium: 355 mg, Fiber: 4 g

Sesame Beef with Broccoli

Another family favorite. I always make sure the skillet is very hot before adding the slices of beef so it's seared properly and stays juicy.

Prep:
30 minutes

Total:
30 minutes

Yield:
Serves 4

- 2 teaspoons reduced-sodium soy sauce
- 1 teaspoon granulated sugar
- 1 teaspoon cornstarch
- 1 clove garlic, minced
- ¾ pound boneless sirloin, cut across the grain into ¼-inch-thick slices

SAUCE
- ½ cup **carrot puree**
- 2 cups low-fat, reduced-sodium beef broth
- 1 tablespoon reduced-sodium soy sauce
- 2 teaspoons cornstarch
- 2 teaspoons sesame oil
- ½-inch piece fresh ginger, peeled and minced
- 2 cloves garlic, minced

- 1 tablespoon olive oil
- 1 pound broccoli, cut into florets, the stems peeled and cut into ½-inch-thick sticks
- ½ cup water
- 1 cup short-grain brown rice, cooked according to the package instructions (makes 4 cups)

1. In a small bowl, stir together the soy sauce, sugar, cornstarch, and garlic. Add the beef and let it marinate for 20 minutes.

2. Make the sauce. In a small bowl, whisk the puree, broth, soy sauce, cornstarch, sesame oil, ginger, and garlic

3. In a large skillet, warm the olive oil over high heat. When the pan is hot, add the beef and marinade. Cook 1 to 2 minutes, until the beef is well seared and no longer pink on the outside, stirring 3 or 4 times. Remove the meat and transfer to a bowl or plate. Reduce the heat to medium and add the broccoli to the pan. Cook 4 to 5 minutes, stirring occasionally.

4. Add the water and cover, cooking 2 to 3 minutes more, until the broccoli is tender but crisp. Pour the sauce over the broccoli. Cook 2 to 3 minutes more, until the sauce thickens. Return the beef to the pan and stir well until combined. Serve immediately with the prepared rice.

Calories: 424, Carbohydrate: 52 g, Protein: 27 g, Total Fat: 12 g, Saturated Fat: 2.5 g, Sodium: 550 mg, Fiber: 6 g

Lo Mein

An easy-to-make version of a great Chinese classic—tastier, healthier, and less greasy. Serve warm or cold with fresh sliced cucumber, a sprinkle of toasted sesame seeds, or even baby corn, which lots of kids seem to love.

QUICK!

Prep:
20 minutes

Total:
20 minutes

Yield:
Serves 4

- 1 (12-ounce) box whole-wheat spaghetti
- ½ cup low-fat, reduced-sodium chicken broth, plus ¼ cup
- ½ cup **sweet potato puree**
- 2 tablespoons reduced-sodium soy sauce
- 1 tablespoon firmly packed dark or light brown sugar
- 1 teaspoon sesame oil
- 2 teaspoons cornstarch
- 2 tablespoons olive oil
- 3 cloves garlic, minced
- 4 green onions, white ends only, thinly sliced
- 4 (6-ounce) center-cut pork chops or cutlets, trimmed of fat and cut across the grain into ¼-inch-thick slices

1. Cook the spaghetti according to the package instructions and set aside. In a medium bowl, whisk the ½ cup of chicken broth, sweet potato puree, soy sauce, brown sugar, sesame oil, and cornstarch. Set aside.

2. Heat the olive oil in a large skillet over medium-high heat. Add the garlic, green onions, and pork. Cook until the garlic and onions become fragrant and the pork begins to brown, 4 to 5 minutes.

3. Add the soy sauce mixture and spaghetti to the skillet. Reduce the heat to low. Cook 1 to 2 minutes more, stirring well, until a thick sauce forms and coats the noodles. Add the remaining chicken broth if the sauce is too thick. Serve immediately.

Sascha:
Baby corn is so cute.

Calories: 673, Carbohydrate: 77 g, Protein: 54 g, Total Fat: 17 g, Saturated Fat: 3 g, Sodium: 470 mg, Fiber: 8 g

Prep:
20 minutes

Total:
55 minutes

Yield:
Serves 4

Orange-Glazed Pork

I love to make this in the early winter, but it's great to make any time of year because it's sweet and tasty and simple to prepare! Serve hot or at room temperature.

GLAZE

- 3 tablespoons orange marmalade
- ½ cup water
- ½ cup **carrot puree**
- 1 tablespoon reduced-sodium soy sauce
- 1 teaspoon chopped fresh ginger
- 2 teaspoons apple cider or white vinegar
- 2 cloves garlic, chopped
- ½ teaspoon cinnamon
- ¼ to ½ teaspoon red pepper flakes or ground cayenne

- 2 pounds pork tenderloin (usually 2 small pieces)
- ½ teaspoon salt
- ¼ teaspoon pepper
- 1 tablespoon olive oil
- ½ cup water

1. Preheat the oven to 400°F. In a medium saucepan, whisk all ingredients for the glaze until smooth. Warm the glaze over medium heat until it begins to bubble. Cook 10 to 15 minutes more, until the liquid is reduced by one quarter and the glaze thickens.

2. Meanwhile, sprinkle the pork loin with salt and pepper. Heat the olive oil in a large ovenproof skillet over high heat. Carefully add the pork and cook 10 minutes, turning once until both sides are browned.

3. Off the heat, add the glaze. Turn the pork once to coat in the glaze. Slide the skillet into the oven and bake until the glaze starts to brown around the inner edges of the skillet, 15 to 20 minutes. Remove the skillet, add the water, and continue to bake 15 to 20 minutes more, until the pork is cooked through and the water has evaporated. Remove the pork to a cutting board and stir the glaze until smooth. Slice the pork and serve with the glaze.

Calories: 341, Carbohydrate: 16 g, Protein: 48 g, Total Fat: 8.5 g, Saturated Fat: 2 g, Sodium: 590 mg, Fiber: 2 g

Salmon Burgers

Make sure the salmon has no pin bones. If it does, pull the bones out with <u>clean</u> pliers—it's actually quite therapeutic. That's the only time-consuming part of this recipe. Otherwise, it's a breeze.

Shown here with Summer Corn Fritters (recipe page 109).

QUICK!

Prep:
15 minutes

Total:
1 hour 25 minutes
(including chill time)

Yield:
Serves 6

- 2 tablespoons chopped fresh ginger
- 2 cloves garlic
- 1 tablespoon reduced-sodium soy sauce
- 2 tablespoons hoisin sauce, plus more to top the burgers, if desired
- 2 tablespoons reduced-fat mayonnaise
- ½ cup **carrot puree**
- ¼ teaspoon salt
- 2 pounds wild salmon, pin bones and skin removed, cut into 1-inch pieces
- 1 teaspoon olive oil
- 6 whole-wheat hamburger buns
- Lettuce and sliced tomato, for garnish (optional)

1. Put the ginger and garlic in a food processor and pulse until finely chopped. Add the soy sauce, hoisin, mayonnaise, carrot puree, salt, and salmon. Pulse until the ingredients are combined and begin to hold together.

2. Form the salmon mixture into 6 patties. (The mixture will be very soft.) Refrigerate for at least 1 hour to firm them up.

3. In a heavy-bottomed skillet over medium heat, brown the burgers in the olive oil, approximately 2 to 3 minutes per side. Serve on toasted buns spread with hoisin sauce and top with lettuce and tomatoes, if desired.

Joy:
Wild salmon is one of the best sources of omega-3 fats. In growing kids, omega-3s are especially important for healthy brain development.

Calories: 394, Carbohydrate: 30 g, Protein: 38 g, Total Fat: 13.5 g, Saturated Fat: 2 g, Sodium: 645 mg, Fiber: 5 g

My Kitchen, My Kids

When my first two children were very small, I saw my kitchen as one big danger zone: the simmering saucepans on the stove, the hot oven, the sharp knives, and my eager kids balancing on chairs in the middle of it all. In my mind, it was a perfect storm of disaster. Besides worrying about safety, there was my sanity. One child inevitably wanted to do what another was doing, like stir the pancake batter instead of cracking the egg. That would lead to a push here, a pull there, and if I didn't catch it in time, a downward spiral into a mini crisis where someone left the kitchen in a huff. All of this to make pancakes together!

But just as my kids have changed as they've grown, so too has my view of them in the kitchen. Over the years, I witnessed with awe the sense of accomplishment and independence they got from "big kid" skills—everything from clearing the table after dinner to washing and drying the dishes. Gradually it dawned on me (as it has on many other moms, I'm sure) that cooking was actually a next logical step in their big-kid development.

Then came the lightning bolt. Shortly after my then eight-year-old daughter started taking a cooking class after school, she excitedly brought home manicotti she had made and devoured it, along with the rest of us, at dinner that night. Two weeks earlier, I had made manicotti and she had raised her eyebrows, pushed her plate away without even trying anything, and sat back in her chair. I realized when she brought *her* version home that it was time to bring my kids into the kitchen with me.

We started slowly, but quickly I realized not only did they enjoy taking ownership of what they had prepared, they were actually interested in how food is grown, harvested, transported, and sold. I soon came to see in my own children what I've since learned—that when children touch food, smell food, and understand the seasons in which these foods grow, they develop an understanding of agriculture, geography, and economics, as well as an overall comfort with these foods when they get to taste them.

I still worry about my kids in the kitchen. We're very careful, and we do follow rules. But we also have a lot of fun. And let's face it: it's a lot harder to say, "I'm not eating that—it's gross!" to a meal that you had a hand in preparing.

Tuna Casserole

Between the tuna, whole-grain wheat, and the puree tucked inside, this is a complete one-pot meal that's packed with nutrition. Serve with a side of raw veggies.

Prep:
30 minutes

Total:
1 hour 30 minutes

Yield:
Serves 6

- Nonstick cooking spray
- 2 tablespoons olive oil
- 2 ribs celery, chopped
- ½ large onion, chopped
- 2 tablespoons whole-wheat flour
- 3 cups nonfat (skim) milk
- 2 (6-ounce) cans light tuna packed in water, drained
- 1½ cups part-skim mozzarella
- 1 cup **carrot puree**
- ½ teaspoon garlic powder
- ¼ teaspoon paprika
- ¼ teaspoon freshly ground black pepper
- 1 pound rice or whole-wheat pasta, such as shells or rotini, cooked according to the package instructions
- ¼ cup whole-grain breadcrumbs

1. Preheat oven to 350°F. Coat an 8 x 12-inch baking dish with cooking spray and set aside. Heat the oil over medium-high heat in a large skillet. Add the celery and onion. Cook 8 to 10 minutes, stirring occasionally, until the vegetables begin to soften but before they brown. Sprinkle the flour over the vegetables and cook 2 to 3 minutes more, until the flour forms a paste around the vegetables. Add 1½ cups of milk and whisk until a thick sauce forms, about 1 to 2 minutes.

2. In a large bowl, mix the remaining milk, the tuna, mozzarella, carrot puree, garlic powder, paprika, and black pepper. Mix with a wooden spoon, breaking up the tuna. Add the vegetables from the skillet, along with the cooked noodles. Stir until well combined.

3. Transfer the noodle mixture into the baking dish and sprinkle with bread-crumbs. Cover with aluminum foil and bake 40 to 45 minutes. Then remove the cover and bake for 15 minutes more to brown. Cool for 15 minutes before serving.

Calories: 562, Carbohydrate: 84 g, Protein: 36 g, Total Fat: 11 g, Saturated Fat: 3.5 g, Sodium: 525 mg, Fiber: 10 g

Shrimp Dumplings

Fun for kids and a really elegant appetizer for grown-ups, these scrumptious dumplings seem special but are easy to make, even with your children. I serve them with low-sodium soy sauce. Topping them with some thinly sliced scallions is also nice.

Prep:
45 minutes

Total:
1 hour 10 minutes

Yield:
Serves 10

- 1 (8-ounce) can sliced water chestnuts, drained
- 3 scallions, white parts only, cut in thirds
- 1 clove garlic, cut in half
- ½-inch piece peeled ginger, cut in thirds
- ½ pound raw medium shrimp, tails and shells removed
- ½ cup **cauliflower puree**
- 1 tablespoon reduced-fat, low-sodium soy sauce
- 1 tablespoon sesame oil
- 1 (12-ounce) package wonton wrappers
- 1 tablespoon olive oil
- Nonstick cooking spray

1. Preheat the oven to 350°F. Place the water chestnuts, scallions, garlic, and ginger in the bowl of a food processor. Pulse until the chestnuts and scallions are finely chopped. Add the shrimp, cauliflower puree, soy sauce, and sesame oil. Pulse 4 or 5 times until the mixture is wet but still chunky.

2. On a flat surface, set out 6 of the wonton wrappers. Dot the centers of each wrapper with a heaping teaspoon of the filling. Drizzle the olive oil onto 2 large baking sheets.

3. Put some water in a small bowl. Using your fingertips, wet the edges of the wrapper with the water and fold the ends together diagonally. Press to seal. Place on the oiled baking sheet and repeat with the remaining wrappers until you have used all the filling.

4. Spray a light coating of cooking spray over the dumplings. Bake 20 to 25 minutes, turning once, until the wontons are crisp and the filling is cooked through.

Jessica:
These days you can find wonton wrappers in the refrigerator or freezer section of any local grocery store.

1 serving = 5 dumplings
Calories: 157, Carbohydrate: 24 g, Protein: 9 g, Total Fat: 3.5 g, Saturated Fat: 0.5 g, Sodium: 290 mg, Fiber: 1 g

Pasta with Pea Pesto

Everyone needs a change from tomato sauce sometimes. I love this cold as a summer lunch or warm for dinner year-round.

QUICK!

Prep:
10 minutes

Total:
25 minutes

Yield:
Serves 6

PESTO

- 2 cups peas (fresh or frozen, blanched in boiling water for 30 seconds and shocked in cold water)
- ½ cup grated Parmesan
- ½ cup pine nuts
- 2 medium cloves garlic
- ¼ cup extra-virgin olive oil
- 2 tablespoons water
- ¼ teaspoon salt

CHICKEN

- 6 boneless, skinless chicken breasts (about 2¼ pounds)
- ½ teaspoon garlic powder
- ¼ teaspoon salt
- ¼ teaspoon pepper
- 1 teaspoon olive oil

- 8 ounces whole-wheat pasta, such as penne or fusilli

1. For the pesto, combine the peas, Parmesan, pine nuts, garlic, olive oil, water, and salt in a food processor. Blend until the ingredients are combined and form a thick sauce.

2. Season the chicken breasts with garlic powder, salt, and pepper. Heat the oil in a skillet over medium heat. Brown the chicken on each side until cooked through, approximately 5 to 6 minutes per side. Cut into 1-inch cubes.

3. Meanwhile, cook pasta according to package directions. Toss together the pasta, pesto, and chicken and serve immediately.

Julian:
I like this with extra Parmesan cheese.

Calories: 567, Carbohydrate: 41 g, Protein: 52 g, Total Fat: 22.5 g, Saturated Fat: 3.5 g, Sodium: 465 mg, Fiber: 6 g

Prep:
20 minutes

Total:
20 minutes

Yield:
Serves 4

Orzo Risotto with Chicken

Thanks to the puree, this is a creamy, rich risotto without the fat. Cauliflower and cream cheese make a lovely combination, enhanced with just a hint of lemon.

- 1 cup whole-wheat orzo pasta
- 1 pound boneless, skinless chicken breasts, thinly sliced
- ½ teaspoon salt
- ¼ teaspoon pepper
- ½ teaspoon sweet paprika
- 2 tablespoons olive oil
- ½ small Vidalia onion, or 1 small yellow onion, chopped
- 2 cloves garlic, finely chopped
- ½ cup low-fat, reduced-sodium chicken broth
- 1 cup **cauliflower puree**
- Zest and juice from 1 large lemon
- ¼ cup reduced-fat cream cheese
- ¼ cup grated Parmesan or Romano cheese

1. Cook the orzo 5 minutes less than the package instructions. Drain and set aside.

2. Sprinkle the chicken with the salt, pepper, and paprika. Heat 1 tablespoon of the olive oil in a large skillet over high heat. Add the chicken and cook until it's brown on the outside and no longer pink in the center, 5 to 6 minutes per side. Remove to a cutting board. When the chicken is cool to the touch, shred it with your fingers. Set aside.

3. In the same skillet, add the remaining tablespoon of olive oil and place over medium heat. Add the onions and garlic. Cook until the onions begin to soften but not brown, 5 to 6 minutes. Stir in the orzo, chicken, broth, and cauliflower puree. Add the lemon zest, cream cheese, and Parmesan or Romano, stirring until the cream cheese melts completely and mixture is creamy. Stir in the lemon juice just before serving.

Joy:
This updated take on the classic comfort food "chicken and rice" delivers great taste without all of the calories, saturated fat, and salt.

Calories: 413, Carbohydrate: 36 g, Protein: 36 g, Total Fat: 13 g, Saturated Fat: 4 g, Sodium: 555 mg, Fiber: 8.5 g

My 5 Favorite Whole-Grain Tips

Whole grains are one of nature's simplest ways of delivering all kinds of good things, from protein to fiber to vitamins and minerals. They're inexpensive, easy to cook, and great to have on hand. And really, there's no need to relearn the way you cook or eat. Adding whole grains to your meals could not be easier.

- Add ½ cup of cooked wild rice, brown rice, or barley to your favorite canned or homemade soup or stew.

- Next time you make meatballs, burgers, or meatloaf, mix ¾ cup of ground bran cereal or flaxseed meal or wheat germ into each pound of ground chicken or turkey.

- Whenever a baking recipe calls for all-purpose flour, substitute half of it with whole-wheat flour.

- Make whole-wheat pretzels or whole-grain crackers the family snack food and serve with hummus, salsa, or bean dip.

- Not many people think of popcorn as a whole grain, but, if prepared healthfully on the stovetop using whole popcorn kernels, it can be one of the healthiest snacks to eat. It's a good source of fiber, has all the benefits of any other whole grain, and is quite filling—all good things for a snack! The best part is that it's low in calories. I'll season it with a little grated cheese and sprinkle with salt or spices, like cayenne pepper or cinnamon.

Prep:
25 minutes

Total:
30 minutes

Yield:
Makes 36 ravioli

Pumpkin Ravioli

Homemade ravioli seems impossible, right? Not at all! This is both the tastiest and the prettiest dish. I love to serve this for a casual meal, and they are so elegant that they work for a fancy dinner party as well.

- 1 (15-ounce) can low-sodium white beans, such as navy, rinsed and drained
- ½ cup canned 100% pure **pumpkin puree**
- ½ cup part-skim ricotta cheese
- ¼ cup grated Parmesan
- ¾ teaspoon garlic powder
- 1 large egg
- 72 wonton wrappers, about 1½ (12-ounce) packages
- 1 tablespoon cornstarch
- 1½ cups jarred marinara sauce, microwaved 1 minute or until warm

1. Fill a large stockpot with water and bring to a boil. Place the beans, pumpkin puree, ricotta, Parmesan, and garlic powder into a food processor. Process until smooth.

2. In a small bowl, beat the egg with about 1 tablespoon of water.

3. Set the wonton wrappers on a cutting board. Place 1 tablespoon of the mixture onto a wrapper. Brush the edges of the wonton with the egg wash. Top off with another wonton sheet. To make a round shape, cut around the base of the pumpkin can. Press the edges of the ravioli together firmly, to seal.

4. Place the ravioli on a baking sheet sprinkled with the cornstarch. When all the ravioli are cut out, carefully place them in the boiling water using a slotted spoon. As soon as they rise, about 4 minutes, they are done. Lift them out with the slotted spoon and divide the ravioli between 6 bowls. Top each portion with ¼ cup marinara sauce and serve immediately.

Julian:

What's inside these ravioli? They taste delicious!

1 serving = 6 ravioli
Calories: 352, Carbohydrate: 62 g, Protein: 15 g, Total Fat: 6 g, Saturated Fat: 2 g, Sodium: 520 mg, Fiber: 5.5 g

Gnocchi

You will not believe how easy this dish is to prepare. These fresh gnocchi are so much creamier and more delicious than store-bought kinds I've tried.

Prep:
40 minutes

Total:
50 minutes

Yield:
Serves 6

- 1 (15-ounce) container part-skim ricotta cheese
- ½ cup **sweet potato puree**
- 1 large egg
- 1 large egg white
- ¼ cup grated Parmesan
- ½ teaspoon baking powder
- ¼ teaspoon salt
- 1 cup whole-wheat pastry flour, plus ¼ cup to roll out the dough
- 1 cup all-purpose flour
- 1 (24-ounce) jarred pasta sauce, heated or at room temperature

1. In a large bowl, mix the ricotta cheese, sweet potato puree, egg, egg white, Parmesan, baking powder, and salt. Add both types of flour at once. Mix with a wooden spoon until the flour is just absorbed, the puree is well combined, and a soft sticky dough forms

2. Cover 2 baking sheets with waxed paper or aluminum foil. Cut the dough into 8 pieces. On a lightly floured counter, roll the dough into a log about 12 inches long and 1 inch thick. Slice off 1 x 1½-inch pieces of dough to form the gnocchi. Transfer to the baking sheet and repeat with remaining dough.

3. Fill an 8-quart stockpot with water and bring to a boil. Add half the gnocchi (so that they don't stick) and gently stir. Cook until the pasta is tender and no longer translucent in the center, 4 to 6 minutes. The gnocchi should be floating. Lift them out with a slotted spoon and transfer to a large serving dish. Cover with aluminum foil. Repeat with the remaining gnocchi and top with sauce. Serve immediately.

Shepherd:
I love to roll the dough!

Calories: 350, Carbohydrate: 50 g, Protein: 18 g, Total Fat: 9 g, Saturated Fat: 4 g, Sodium: 645 mg, Fiber: 6 g

Prep:
30 minutes

Total:
35 minutes

Yield:
Serves 4

Fettuccine Alfredo

Cauliflower is the perfect addition to this classic white sauce. Not only does it add to the creaminess without the fat, but it also helps keep the sauce smooth. A little friend of our family claims he only likes "plain pasta with nothing on it"—but he loves to eat this.

- 12 ounces whole-wheat fettuccine
- 2 tablespoons trans-fat-free soft tub margarine spread
- 2 cloves garlic, minced
- 2 tablespoons whole-wheat flour
- 1 cup nonfat (skim) milk
- ¾ cup grated reduced-fat (2%) sharp cheddar or part-skim mozzarella cheese
- ½ cup **cauliflower puree**
- ¼ cup grated Parmesan
- ¼ teaspoon salt
- ¼ teaspoon pepper
- ¼ teaspoon sweet paprika
- 1 to 2 sprigs fresh basil (optional)

1. Cook the pasta according to package instructions. Reserve ½ cup of the cooking water, then strain the pasta. Set aside.

2. Heat the margarine in a large skillet with deep sides over medium heat. When the margarine foams, add the garlic. Cook until the garlic is fragrant but does not brown, 1 to 2 minutes. Add the flour and cook 4 to 5 minutes, mashing the flour into the margarine until it forms a smooth paste.

3. Add ¼ cup of the milk at a time and whisk constantly until the milk is absorbed and a creamy sauce starts to form. Once all the milk is incorporated, bring the sauce to a slow boil, whisking 1 minute more.

4. Stir in the cheddar or mozzarella, the cauliflower puree, and Parmesan, mixing until smooth, about 1 to 2 minutes. Add the salt, pepper, paprika, and pasta. Toss to coat. Add a little of the reserved pasta water if the mixture is too thick. Top with a sprig or two of fresh basil, if using, and serve immediately.

Sascha:
I love this pasta!
It's so buttery-tasting!

Calories: 500, Carbohydrate: 72 g, Protein: 25 g, Total Fat: 14 g, Saturated Fat: 4.5 g, Sodium: 525 mg, Fiber: 16 g

Other Mothers Know Best!

Sarah, mother of Amanda (5):

My kids were drinking way too much juice and sweetened drinks. They found water "boring." Now I freeze fruit juice in ice cube trays and add a few "juice cubes" to seltzer or water for a little sweetness. They love the taste and all the different-colored cubes.

Deirdre, mother of Nathan (3) and Jeremy (6):

I refuse to buy those sugar cereals my kids see (and subsequently want!) on TV. Instead, I allow them to add their own sugar to an unsweetened cereal. You'd be surprised at how little sugar is needed to add some sweetness, especially when compared to what goes into those on the supermarket shelves. A half-teaspoonful of sugar sprinkled on top will look and feel like a lot when kids get to spoon it on themselves.

Prep:
20 minutes

Total:
40 minutes

Yield:
Serves 8

Macaroni and Cheese

To me, there's nothing more comforting or universally crowd-pleasing than mac and cheese. It's a staple at our home year-round, and apparently at many other homes, too. So for all the readers of Deceptively Delicious that asked for another version, here it is!

- 1 pound whole-wheat pasta, such as elbows or shells
- Nonstick cooking spray
- 2 tablespoons trans-fat-free soft tub margarine spread
- 1½ tablespoons flour
- 2½ cups nonfat (skim) milk
- 1 cup shredded reduced-fat (2%) cheddar cheese
- 1 teaspoon salt
- ½ cup **carrot** or **sweet potato puree**
- ¼ cup whole-wheat breadcrumbs
- 2 tablespoons grated Parmesan

1. Bring a large pot of salted water to a boil. Add the pasta and cook according to package directions until al dente.

2. Preheat the oven to 375°F. Coat a 9 x 12-inch baking dish with cooking spray.

3. Heat the margarine in a heavy-bottomed saucepan. Whisk in the flour to combine. Slowly whisk in milk to prevent lumps from forming. Bring to a boil and cook until the mixture thickens slightly, about 5 minutes. Add the cheddar cheese, salt, and carrot puree. Whisk until smooth. Stir the cheese mixture into the pasta.

4. Transfer to a baking dish. Sprinkle the top with breadcrumbs and Parmesan. Bake until the macaroni and cheese is bubbly and the breadcrumbs begin to brown, 20 minutes.

Joy:

No powdered cheese sauce here! This recipe uses reduced-fat cheese, which provides a healthy dose of creamy calcium while cutting out some of the saturated fat.

With carrot puree:
Calories: 330, Carbohydrate: 53 g,
Protein: 16 g, Total Fat: 7 g, Saturated Fat: 3 g,
Sodium: 545 mg, Fiber: 6 g

With sweet potato puree:
Calories: 335, Carbohydrate: 55 g,
Protein: 16 g, Total Fat: 7 g, Saturated Fat: 3 g,
Sodium: 540 mg, Fiber: 6 g

Prep:
20 minutes

Total:
50 minutes

Yield:
Serves 4

Chicken Cannelloni

This quick and delicious meal looks like you spent hours slaving away, when in fact the prep takes no time at all.

- 8 whole-wheat lasagna sheets, (4 x 4 inches or 3 x 6 inches)
- Nonstick cooking spray
- 1 pound boneless, skinless chicken breasts, cooked and thinly shredded
- ¾ cup part-skim ricotta cheese
- ¾ cup **cauliflower puree**
- ¼ cup grated Parmesan
- 1 teaspoon garlic powder
- ¼ teaspoon salt
- 2 cups jarred tomato sauce
- 1 cup shredded part-skim mozzarella

1. Boil and salt the water for lasagna sheets. Cook, drain, and then place the lasagna in a bowl of cool water.

2. Preheat the oven to 350°F. Coat an 9 x 12-inch dish with cooking spray.

3. In a large bowl, mix the chicken, ricotta, cauliflower puree, Parmesan, garlic powder, and salt until the chicken is well coated.

4. Place 1 lasagna sheet on the cutting board. On the edge closest to you, spread out ¼ cup of the filling so that it covers one third of the sheet. With your fingertips, roll the lasagna into a tube (lift the edge of the pasta with filling and roll). Transfer seam-side down to the baking dish. Repeat with the remaining sheets. Pour the sauce around the cannelloni but not on top. Sprinkle with mozzarella and bake, uncovered, 25 to 30 minutes.

Jessica:
This is a great meal to prepare the night before and bake the next day after work.

1 serving = 2 cannelloni
Calories: 510, Carbohydrate: 57 g, Protein: 47 g, Total Fat: 12 g, Saturated Fat: 6 g, Sodium: 850 mg, Fiber: 9 g

Prep:
20 minutes

Total:
45 minutes

Yield:
Serves 6

Ellen's Baked Ziti

Growing up, my mom would prepare this dish at night after my sisters and I went to bed. The next day I would put it in the oven for her so dinner would be ready when she got home from work. Some steamed veggies and an easy salad are great on the side.

- 14 ounces whole-wheat ziti
- 2 cups jarred tomato sauce
- ½ cup **carrot puree**
- 1 cup part-skim ricotta cheese
- ½ cup cauliflower puree
- 2 large egg whites
- 1 cup shredded part-skim mozzarella
- 2 cloves garlic, finely chopped
- ¼ teaspoon pepper
- ¼ cup grated Parmesan

1. Preheat the oven to 450°F. Cook the pasta a few minutes less than the package instructions indicate so that it will still be firm when baked. Drain and set aside.

2. Pour the tomato sauce into a medium bowl. Add the carrot puree and mix until well combined.

3. In another small bowl, combine the ricotta, cauliflower puree, egg whites, ½ cup of the mozzarella, garlic, and pepper.

4. Spread about half of the tomato sauce onto the bottom of a glass pan or casserole dish. Then add a layer with half the pasta. Spoon the ricotta mixture on top and cover with the rest of the pasta. Top it off with remaining sauce. Then sprinkle with the Parmesan and remaining mozzarella. Bake for about 30 minutes, until the cheese starts to brown and the filling is hot. Or cover with aluminum foil, refrigerate, and bake the next day.

Shepherd:
I love when Grandma Ellen makes this for us.

Calories: 413, Carbohydrate: 66 g, Protein: 22 g, Total Fat: 8.5 g, Saturated Fat: 4.5 g, Sodium: 520 mg, Fiber: 2.5 g

Prep:
20 minutes

Total:
1 hour

Yield:
Serves 8

Creamy Whole-Grain Risotto

Much easier than regular risotto because the creaminess of the puree means it doesn't require constant stirring. It goes without saying that it's also much lower in fat and calories.

- 2 cups short-grain brown rice
- 2 tablespoons olive oil
- 1 large onion, chopped
- 4 cloves garlic, chopped
- 2 cups low-fat, reduced-sodium vegetable or chicken broth
- 1 cup **cauliflower puree**
- 1 cup **carrot puree**
- 1 sprig fresh basil
- ½ teaspoon salt
- ¼ teaspoon pepper
- 2 tablespoons trans-fat-free soft tub margarine spread
- ½ cup grated Parmesan

1. In a medium saucepan, add the brown rice and 4 cups of water. Bring to a boil. Immediately cover and reduce to a low simmer. Cook until the rice is tender, 40 to 45 minutes. Turn the heat off and let the rice steam with the lid on for 5 minutes. Drain the rice and set aside.

2. Meanwhile, heat the oil in a large skillet over medium-high heat. When the oil is hot, add the onion and garlic. Cook 8 to 10 minutes, stirring occasionally, until the onions begin to soften but not brown. Add the rice, broth, both purees, basil, salt, and pepper. Simmer on low heat for 5 minutes more, until one quarter of the liquid evaporates. Off the heat, stir in the margarine and remove the basil. Sprinkle with Parmesan and serve immediately.

Calories: 285, Carbohydrate: 44 g, Protein: 7 g, Total Fat: 9 g, Saturated Fat: 2 g, Sodium: 315 mg, Fiber: 4 g

Summer Corn Fritters

My kids go crazy when I make these, because they make the house smell like french fries.

Photograph page 86.

Prep:
15 minutes

Total:
35 minutes

Yield:
Serves 12

- 1 cup medium-ground yellow cornmeal
- ½ cup whole-wheat pastry flour
- 2 teaspoons baking powder
- ¼ teaspoon garlic powder
- ¼ teaspoon salt
- ¼ teaspoon pepper
- 1 cup **carrot** or **cauliflower puree**
- 1 cup low-fat (1%) buttermilk
- 4 slices low-sodium ham, chopped (about ¾ cup), if desired
- ½ cup corn kernels, defrosted if frozen, or fresh from 1 ear of corn
- 2 scallions, white part only, chopped
- 2 large egg whites
- 2 tablespoons honey
- 2 tablespoons olive oil

1. In a large bowl, mix the cornmeal, flour, baking powder, garlic powder, salt, and pepper.

2. Make a well in the center of the cornmeal mixture with a wooden spoon. In the center of the well, place the carrot or cauliflower puree, buttermilk, ham if using, corn, scallions, egg whites, and honey. Mix the wet ingredients together in the well, slowly combining the corn mixture until just combined, about 10 turns with a wooden spoon. Batter will be lumpy.

3. Heat 1 tablespoon of the olive oil in a large skillet over medium-high heat. Drop ¼ cupfuls of batter into the skillet about 1 inch apart. Cook until golden, 4 to 5 minutes per side, and transfer to a plate. Repeat with the remaining tablespoon of olive oil and batter. Serve immediately.

Jessica:

Cooking these in a cast-iron skillet makes them even more crispy and perfect. I use an ice-cream scoop to transfer the batter to the skillet.

With carrot puree:
1 serving = 1 fritter
Calories: 129, Carbohydrate: 25 g,
Protein: 4 g, Total Fat: 3 g, Saturated Fat: 0.5 g,
Sodium: 180 mg, Fiber: 2 g

With cauliflower puree:
1 serving = 1 fritter
Calories: 121, Carbohydrate: 23 g,
Protein: 4 g, Total Fat: 3 g, Saturated Fat: 0.5 g,
Sodium: 165 mg, Fiber: 1.5 g

Black Bean Burgers

A great meatless meal that is not just for vegetarians. Meat eaters love these hearty, flavorful burgers too!

Shown here with Corn Bread (recipe page 122).

Prep:
20 minutes

Total:
30 minutes

Yield:
Serves 6

- ½ cup onion, chopped
- 2 cloves garlic, minced
- 1½ cups mixed vegetables, such as squash, zucchini, peppers, portabella mushrooms, and corn, diced
- 3 teaspoons olive oil
- 2 (15-ounce) cans low-sodium black beans, drained and rinsed
- 1 large egg
- 1 cup whole-wheat breadcrumbs
- ¼ teaspoon salt
- 1 teaspoon pepper
- 1 teaspoon chili powder
- 6 whole-wheat sandwich buns

1. Sauté the onion, garlic, and vegetables in 1 teaspoon of the olive oil until the vegetables soften.

2. Combine the sautéed vegetables, black beans, egg, breadcrumbs, salt, pepper, and chili powder in the bowl of an electric mixer. Using a paddle, blend until some of the beans are broken up and the mixture begins to hold together. Form the mixture into 6 patties.

3. Sauté the patties in the remaining 2 teaspoons of olive oil until browned, approximately 2 to 3 minutes per side. Serve on toasted sandwich buns.

Jerry:
*These are fantastic!
And I am a hamburger lover.*

Calories: 387, Carbohydrate: 68 g, Protein: 20 g, Total Fat: 5.5 g, Saturated Fat: 0.5 g, Sodium: 630 mg, Fiber: 17 g

Whole-Grain Winter Salads

As someone who loves vegetables, I eat lots of salads. During winter, when so little is in season where I live, it can be difficult to come up with appealing and fresh-tasting ideas. One way to adjust to the months—and to "winterize" salads a bit—is by using whole grains. Simply adding healthy grains makes salads more interesting and turns them into complete meals, low in fat and high in good things like protein, fiber, carbohydrates, and vitamins. As an added bonus, these salads keep well in your fridge for days!

Wheatberry is easy to cook and has a great shape and mild flavor. Try a salad of grated carrot and fennel, some raisins or diced apples, and a few toasted pecans or walnuts with cooked wheatberries. Add a little orange zest to an oil and vinegar dressing to liven things up.

Farro has a mild, almost nutty flavor. Farro is used quite a bit in Italy, which is where I first tried it, at a restaurant in Forte dei Marmi, Italy. The salad was made with cubed baked butternut squash, peas (you can use frozen), and sliced red onion, topped with a light vinaigrette.

Quinoa is a perfect little protein food, light and fluffy and easy to use hot or cold. It goes beautifully with chopped red pepper, feta cheese, black beans, scallions, and some chopped cilantro or parsley. Add a bit of good olive oil and a squeeze of lime.

Rice Pilaf

Using brown rice and cauliflower puree makes a very healthy version of a pilaf. I serve it with almost any chicken, fish, or beef dish.

Photograph page 66.

Photograph page 66.

QUICK!

Prep:
5 minutes

Total:
50 minutes

Yield:
Serves 5

- 2 cloves garlic, chopped
- 1 teaspoon olive oil
- 1 cup brown rice
- ½ cup **cauliflower puree**
- 1¼ cups low-fat, reduced-sodium chicken broth
- ¼ teaspoon salt

1. In a heavy-bottomed saucepan, sauté the garlic in the olive oil until it just begins to turn golden on the edges. Add the uncooked rice and toss to coat, approximately 30 seconds.

2. Add the cauliflower puree, chicken broth, and salt. Cover and bring to a boil. Turn the heat down to a simmer and cook with the lid tightly in place, approximately 45 minutes, or until the rice is tender. Do not stir!

3. Let the rice stand 5 minutes. Fluff with a fork and serve.

Shepherd, Sascha, and Julian:
This is our favorite rice. We could eat it every night!

Calories: 154, Carbohydrate: 30 g, Protein: 4 g, Total Fat: 2 g, Saturated Fat: 0.5 g, Sodium: 140 mg, Fiber: 2 g

Prep:
15 minutes

Total:
30 minutes

Yield:
Serves 6

Cauliflower Gratin

I got my kids eating whole cauliflower because of this miracle recipe! I also make a broccoli version the same way.

Photograph page 57.

- 1 medium head cauliflower
- 1 tablespoon trans-fat-free soft tub margarine spread
- 2 teaspoons flour (all-purpose or whole-wheat)
- 1 cup nonfat (skim) milk
- ½ cup reduced-fat (2%) shredded cheddar cheese
- ½ cup **butternut squash** or **carrot puree**
- ½ teaspoon salt
- ¼ teaspoon pepper
- 2 tablespoons grated Parmesan

1. Preheat the oven to 400°F. Bring a medium saucepan of salted water to a boil. Cut the cauliflower into bite-size florets. Blanch for 2 to 3 minutes so that they just begin to get tender but are still firm. Drain in a colander and set aside.

2. In the same saucepan, melt the margarine. Whisk in the flour and cook 1 minute over medium heat. Slowly whisk in the milk to prevent lumps from forming and bring to a boil. The mixture will begin to thicken. Cook 2 to 3 minutes more. Reduce the heat to low and add the cheddar, butternut squash or carrot puree, salt, and pepper.

3. Add the cauliflower to the cheese mixture and transfer to a greased 9-inch baking dish. Top with grated Parmesan. Bake for 15 minutes until the gratin is bubbly and the top begins to brown. Serve immediately.

Joy:
Cauliflower is from the Cruciferous family, just like broccoli, and has many of the same cancer-fighting nutrients ... but a much milder flavor.

With carrot puree:
Calories: 102, Carbohydrate: 11 g,
Protein: 7 g, Total Fat: 4.5 g, Saturated Fat: 1.5 g,
Sodium: 385 mg, Fiber: 3 g

With squash puree:
Calories: 102, Carbohydrate: 11 g,
Protein: 7 g, Total Fat: 4.5 g, Saturated Fat: 1.5 g,
Sodium: 370 mg, Fiber: 3 g

Sautéed Spinach with Raisins and Pine Nuts

My friend Bruce has a restaurant that makes the most delicious creamed spinach with nutmeg in it. This is my version!

QUICK!

Prep:
20 minutes

Total:
25 minutes

Yield:
Serves 4

- ⅓ cup raisins
- ¼ cup reduced-fat, low-sodium chicken broth
- 6 tablespoons pine nuts
- 1 tablespoon olive oil
- 1 (12-ounce) package of baby spinach, rinsed and squeezed dry
- ¼ teaspoon salt
- ¼ teaspoon pepper
- ½ teaspoon freshly grated nutmeg
- ¼ teaspoon cinnamon
- 2 tablespoons reduced-fat sour cream

1. Place the raisins and chicken broth in a small glass bowl. Heat in the microwave for 30 seconds to plump the raisins. Drain the raisins and reserve the liquid. Set aside.

2. Heat a large skillet over medium-high heat. Add the pine nuts and toast 10 to 15 minutes, stirring occasionally, until the nuts begin to brown. Reduce heat if the pine nuts begin to burn.

3. Increase the heat to high. Pour the olive oil over the pine nuts. Add half the spinach, the salt, pepper, nutmeg, and cinnamon. Press the spinach down with a small pot lid until it wilts, about 1 to 2 minutes. Add the rest of the spinach when there is enough space in the pan. Continue to cook 1 to 2 minutes more, until all the spinach is wilted but does not brown. If the spinach is too dry or starts to brown, add a little of the reserved liquid. Cool slightly before stirring in the raisins and sour cream, then serve immediately.

Shepherd:
I love spinach! I love it plain or the creamy and crunchy kind my mom makes.

Calories: 187, Carbohydrate: 15 g, Protein: 5 g, Total Fat: 13.5 g, Saturated Fat: 2 g, Sodium: 220 mg, Fiber: 3 g

Huevos Rancheros

I serve this for Sunday brunch or lunch—especially on Father's Day.

Shown here with Watermelon Punch (recipe page 186).

(recipe page 186)

Prep:
20 minutes

Total:
20 minutes

Yield:
Serves 6

- 1 tablespoon olive oil
- 1 small red onion, chopped
- 1 small yellow onion, chopped
- 1 (15-ounce) can low-sodium black beans or red kidney beans, drained and rinsed
- 2 teaspoons ground cumin
- ½ cup **cauliflower puree**
- ½ cup salsa
- 6 (8-inch) whole-wheat soft tortillas
- Nonstick cooking spray
- 6 tablespoons shredded reduced-fat (2%) cheddar cheese
- 1 to 2 tablespoons chopped pickled jalapeños
- 6 medium eggs
- 6 tablespoons fat-free sour cream

1. Add the olive oil to a medium sauté pan. Add both onions and sauté for 2 to 3 minutes until soft. Add the beans and cumin. Stir in the puree, then the salsa. Cook together until all the ingredients are hot and the flavors combine.

2. Set a small skillet over medium-high heat. When the pan is hot, coat a tortilla with a light layer of cooking spray. Brown the tortilla until it becomes crispy, turning once, 1 to 2 minutes. Repeat with the remaining tortillas.

3. Place the tortillas on individual plates. Divide the bean mixture evenly between them and top with 1 tablespoon of shredded cheese and jalapeños.

4. In the same pan as the tortillas, fry each egg until done to your liking—over easy, medium, or hard—using a light coating of cooking spray. You can also scramble them. Place the eggs on top of the cheese on the tortillas. Top each tortilla with 1 tablespoon of the sour cream.

Jerry:
I love the crunchy tortilla on the bottom.

Calories: 322, Carbohydrate: 44 g, Protein: 19 g, Total Fat: 12 g, Saturated Fat: 2.5 g, Sodium: 695 mg, Fiber: 14 g

Cheese Nachos

I make these for my husband and his friends when they are watching sports on T.V. This hearty dish is always a huge hit and often requested, especially by Jerry's friend George Wallace.

Prep:
20 minutes

Total:
20 minutes

Yield:
Serves 6

- Nonstick cooking spray
- 1 pound extra-lean ground turkey breast
- 2 teaspoons ground cumin
- 2 teaspoons chili powder
- 1½ teaspoons garlic powder
- ½ teaspoon salt
- ½ teaspoon dried oregano
- ½ cup **cauliflower puree**
- 1 tablespoon "no salt added" tomato paste
- 1 tablespoon olive oil
- 2 tablespoons whole-wheat flour
- 1 cup nonfat (skim) milk
- ½ cup **carrot puree**
- ¾ cup grated reduced-fat (2%) cheddar cheese
- 2-3 teaspoons chopped pickled jalapeños
- 6 ounces baked tortilla chips
- ¼ cup jarred mild tomato salsa

1. Set a large skillet over high heat. Coat with a thin layer of cooking spray and add the turkey. Sprinkle the turkey with the cumin, chili powder, 1 teaspoon of the garlic powder, salt, and oregano. Cook until the turkey begins to brown and is cooked through, 4 to 5 minutes. Off the heat, add the cauliflower puree and tomato paste, stirring well to combine. Set aside.

2. Heat the oil in a small saucepan over medium-high heat. Add the flour and cook 2 to 3 minutes, stirring occasionally until a thick paste forms. Increase the heat to high and add the milk. Whisk vigorously and bring to a boil. Reduce to a simmer and whisk in the carrot puree, cheddar cheese, jalapeños, and the remaining ½ teaspoon of garlic powder, stirring 1 minute until the cheese is melted.

3. Place the tortilla chips on a large platter. Spoon the turkey mixture and salsa over the chips, then pour the cheese mixture on top. If you wish, you can heat the chips first in the oven, on an oven-safe pan.

Sascha:
My brothers and I like to eat nachos while we watch sports with our dad.

Calories: 298, Carbohydrate: 34 g, Protein: 27 g, Total Fat: 7 g, Saturated Fat: 2 g, Sodium: 680 mg, Fiber: 4 g

Skinny Egg Salad

These ingredients are always stocked in my kitchen, so I'll often make this for lunch in a pinch. My grandmother used to make me egg salad when I was little. This version is far less fattening and just as good.

QUICK!

Prep:
20 minutes

Total:
25 minutes

Yield:
Serves 4

- 1 dozen large eggs
- 4 green onions
- 6 tablespoons reduced-fat mayonnaise
- ¼ cup nonfat plain yogurt
- ½ cup **cauliflower puree**
- 1 teaspoon Dijon mustard
- ¼ teaspoon pepper
- Pinch or 2 of sweet paprika
- 8 slices whole-wheat sandwich bread

1. Place the eggs in a large saucepan. Cover completely with cold water. Bring to a boil, then remove from the heat. Cover and let the eggs rest 15 minutes. Drain the eggs, peel, and cut in half. Chop all of the whites and 4 yolks, discard the rest.

2. Thinly slice the white part of the green onions and place in a large bowl. Add the mayonnaise, yogurt, cauliflower puree, and mustard.

3. Gently stir in the eggs and yolks, and add the pepper and paprika.

4. Divide the filling evenly on top of 4 slices of bread. Top with the remaining slices of bread and serve.

Shepherd:
Sometimes my mom puts this in a pita pocket for me.

Calories: 349, Carbohydrate: 33 g, Protein: 23 g, Total Fat: 14 g, Saturated Fat: 2.5 g, Sodium: 750 mg, Fiber: 5 g

Prep:
10 minutes

Total:
30 minutes

Yield:
Serves 12

Corn Bread

We are a corn bread family. We love it. Period. I serve it with eggs and black beans for breakfast, spicy grilled chicken for lunch or dinner, and Jerry and the kids love it as a snack, too.

Photograph page 110.

- Nonstick cooking spray
- 1½ cups fine ground cornmeal
- ½ cup all-purpose flour
- ½ cup whole-wheat flour
- 1 tablespoon baking powder
- ½ teaspoon salt
- 1 cup of nonfat (skim) milk
- ½ cup **carrot puree**
- 2 tablespoons pure maple syrup
- ¼ cup light olive oil or canola oil
- 2 large eggs

1. Preheat the oven to 400°F. Spray a 9 x 9-inch square pan or 9-inch round baking pan with cooking spray.

2. In a mixing bowl, whisk the cornmeal, flours, baking powder, and salt until well combined. In a small bowl, whisk together the milk, carrot puree, maple syrup, oil, and eggs. Add the liquid to the flour mixture and stir until just combined—there may still be some unmixed flour or cornmeal. Don't overmix.

3. Pour the batter into the sprayed pan and bake until lightly browned, 20 to 25 minutes. The corn bread is cooked when a cake tester (or toothpick) inserted into the center comes out clean. If the top begins to brown too much, cover with a small sheet of aluminum foil and finish baking.

Sascha:
I like to have jam on my corn bread.

Calories: 57, Carbohydrate: 8.5 g, Protein: 1.5 g, Total Fat: 2 g, Saturated Fat: 0 g, Sodium: 62 mg, Fiber: 0.5 g

French Dressing

A healthier and tastier version than the bottled kind, made with carrot puree. One of my friends loves to serve this dressing on top of long stems of crunchy romaine lettuce.

Photograph page 124.

Prep:
10 minutes

Total:
10 minutes

Yield:
¾ cup

- ½ cup **carrot puree**
- 2 tablespoons ketchup
- 2 tablespoons reduced-fat mayonnaise
- Juice of 1 large lemon (about 2 tablespoons)
- 1 tablespoon canola oil
- 1 tablespoon water
- 1 clove garlic, minced
- ¼ teaspoon salt
- ½ teaspoon sweet paprika
- ½ teaspoon garlic powder
- ½ teaspoon onion powder

1. Combine all the ingredients in a mini-chopper and blend until smooth. Store, refrigerated, in an airtight container for up to 1 week.

1 serving = 2 tablespoons
Calories: 55, Carbohydrate: 5 g, Protein: 0.5 g, Total Fat: 4 g, Saturated Fat: 0.5 g, Sodium: 210 mg, Fiber: 1 g

Caesar Dressing

QUICK!

Prep:
10 minutes

Total:
10 minutes

Yield:
1 cup

I love that you can reduce fat by using cauliflower puree and still maintain all the flavor of a good Caesar dressing. This dressing helped me get my kids to enjoy salad. Shown here with French and Thousand Island Dressings (recipes pages 123 and 126).

- ¾ cup **cauliflower puree**
- ¼ cup grated Parmesan
- Juice of 1 large lemon (about 2 tablespoons)
- 2 tablespoons water
- 1 tablespoon olive oil
- ¼ teaspoon salt
- 1 clove garlic, finely minced
- ½ teaspoon low-sodium Worcestershire sauce
- ½ teaspoon hot sauce (such as Tabasco)
- ¼ teaspoon pepper

1. Place all the ingredients in a mini-chopper and blend until smooth. Store in an airtight container, refrigerated, 4 to 5 days.

Sascha:
I love romaine lettuce because it's crunchy. This dressing is so good on top.

1 serving = 2 tablespoons
Calories: 32, Carbohydrate: 1.5 g, Protein: 1.5 g, Total Fat: 2.5 g, Saturated Fat: 0.5 g, Sodium: 120 mg, Fiber: 0.5 g

Prep:
10 minutes

Total:
10 minutes

Yield:
1 cup

Thousand Island Dressing

The butternut squash puree gives this dressing more goodness than the store-bought kind, which is often high in calories, sodium, and preservatives.

Photograph page 124.

- 1 large egg, hard-boiled
- ½ cup **butternut squash puree**
- 2 tablespoons reduced-fat mayonnaise
- 2 tablespoons reduced-fat sour cream
- 1 pickle, cut in thirds
- 1 teaspoon chili sauce
- ¼ teaspoon salt
- ¼ teaspoon sweet paprika
- ½ teaspoon garlic powder

1. Peel the hard-boiled egg and discard the yolk.

2. Place the white in a mini-chopper, along with the butternut squash puree, mayonnaise, sour cream, pickle, chili sauce, salt, paprika, and garlic powder. Blend until smooth.

3. Store, refrigerated, in an airtight container for up to 5 days.

1 serving = 2 tablespoons
Calories: 38, Carbohydrate: 3 g, Protein: 1 g, Total Fat: 2 g, Saturated Fat: 0.5 g, Sodium: 200 mg, Fiber: 1 g

Dessert

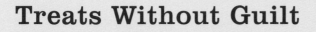

Treats Without Guilt

I have included a nice-sized dessert section in this book. I love sweets, and judging by the enthusiasm and interest readers had in the dessert section of my first book, I am not alone. Homemade treats are better for you, more economical, and far more delicious than store-bought ones—and making them can be a fun activity alone or with your kids.

I would also venture to say that treats are an important part of good eating. If you keep your ingredients wholesome, watch the amount of sugar and saturated fat you cook with, and control your portion size, then having a treat should be completely enjoyable. In fact, if you enjoy your treats without guilt, it is a surefire way to stay on track with healthy, balanced eating. Deprivation always leads down the wrong path.

So, I say, enjoy the right foods, indulge in moderation, and love every minute of it! And with that, I give you the following pages.

Julian:
I love to make chocolate-chip cookies with my mom because there are a lot of fun jobs I can do, like measuring the flour and cracking the eggs, which I am getting really good at.

Sascha:
I love to make the doughnut cookies because it is like playing with Play-Doh when I get to roll out the dough with my fingers.

Chocolate Bread Pudding

I am cherry-crazy. Add them to chocolate and bread? Heaven!
I use enormous self-control to spoon out only one cup for
each serving.

Prep:
25 minutes

Total:
1 hour 10 minutes

Yield:
Serves 8

- Nonstick cooking spray
- 3 cups nonfat (skim) milk
- 6 tablespoons unsweetened cocoa powder
- ½ cup firmly packed light brown sugar
- 1 cup **carrot puree**
- 8 ounces soft whole-wheat bread, cubed (about 10 cups)
- ½ cup dried cherries
- 2 large egg whites
- 1 large egg
- 2 teaspoons pure vanilla extract
- 2 teaspoons pure almond extract

1. Preheat the oven to 375°F. Coat a 1-pound loaf pan or 8 x 8-inch square baking dish with cooking spray.

2. In a small saucepan, whisk the milk, cocoa powder, and sugar. Bring the milk mixture to a near boil. Remove from the heat. Pour into a large bowl and stir in the carrot puree. Add the bread and stir to coat. Soak for 10 to 15 minutes, until the milk mixture cools enough to touch.

3. Add the cherries, egg whites, egg, vanilla, and almond extracts. Stir well, until the eggs are incorporated and the liquid becomes smooth and coats the bread.

4. Transfer to the baking pan and bake until the bread pudding is crusty on top and puffy in the center, 45 to 50 minutes.

Shepherd:
I love to pick the cherries out of the chocolate and eat them first.

Calories: 234, Carbohydrate: 46 g, Protein: 10 g, Total Fat: 2.5 g, Saturated Fat: 0.5 g, Sodium: 220 mg, Fiber: 5 g

Chocolate Yogurt Cheesecake

This seemingly decadent dessert always gets the same response: "There is NO WAY this is low-fat. It's too good!" The graham cracker and hazelnut crust couldn't be simpler to make.

Prep:
20 minutes

Total:
3 hours
(including chill time)

Yield:
Serves 12

- ½ cup hazelnuts or hazelnut pieces
- 6 graham cracker squares, or 1 cup graham cracker crumbs
- 1 teaspoon cinnamon
- 2 tablespoons canola oil
- 3 large egg whites
- ¼ teaspoon salt
- 1½ cups low-fat plain Greek yogurt
- ½ cup nonfat sour cream
- 3 tablespoons unsweetened cocoa
- ¾ cup firmly packed dark brown sugar
- ½ cup **carrot puree**
- 6 tablespoons all-purpose flour
- 2 teaspoons pure vanilla extract

1. Preheat the oven to 325°F. Place the hazelnuts in a food processor and finely chop. Break up the graham crackers and add them to the nuts, along with the cinnamon. Process into fine crumbs. Add the oil and pulse 2 to 3 times, until the graham crackers are moist. Press the graham cracker mixture into the bottom of an 8-inch-round deep-dish pie plate or an 8-inch springform pan.

2. Place the egg whites and salt in a large, clean metal bowl. With a mixer on high, beat the egg whites until they are fluffy and cling to the bowl when tilted, about 2 minutes. Set aside.

3. In another large bowl, whisk the yogurt, sour cream, cocoa, brown sugar, carrot puree, flour, and vanilla. With a rubber spatula, fold in the egg whites in 3 batches. Pour the batter over the crust and smooth with a rubber spatula.

4. Bake until the edges are slightly browned but the center is still soft and wobbles when the pan is moved, 35 to 40 minutes. Transfer to a wire rack and allow to cool before removing from the pan. Cover and chill for 2 hours before serving.

Calories: 195, Carbohydrate: 28 g, Protein: 6 g, Total Fat: 7 g, Saturated Fat: 1 g, Sodium: 135 mg, Fiber: 2 g

Maple Peanut Butter Fondue

To make fruit for dessert more exciting, I portion out little bowls of this fondue (about ¼ cup each) for dipping. It'll stay fresh in the fridge for a week or more, but it'll be gone before that!

QUICK!

Prep:
10 minutes

Total:
15 minutes

Yield:
Serves 12

- 1 cup pure maple syrup
- 1 cup natural peanut butter (creamy)
- 1 teaspoon pure vanilla extract
- ½ cup **cauliflower puree**
- ½ cup **yellow squash puree**
- 6 cups fruit, cut into 1-inch slices, such as apples, bananas, pineapple, mango, strawberries, or grapes.

1. Combine the maple syrup and peanut butter in a heavy-bottomed saucepan. Cook over medium heat, whisking until smooth. Add the vanilla and the cauliflower and squash purees, then stir to combine.

2. Serve with sliced fruit.

   Note: For the creamiest results, use a peanut butter that doesn't separate and require stirring.

Shepherd, Sascha, and Julian:
We use toothpicks to dip!

Calories: 236, Carbohydrate: 33 g, Protein: 5.5 g, Total Fat: 11 g, Saturated Fat: 2.5 g, Sodium: 105 mg, Fiber: 3 g

Prep:
30 minutes

Total:
1 hour 15 minutes

Yield:
Serves 12

Apple Crumble

Every fall, we go to a great orchard in Long Island, New York, and pick tons of apples. I make this apple crumble with the ones we can't finish.

- Nonstick cooking spray

FILLING

- 4 large Golden Delicious or Gala apples (about 3 pounds)
- ½ cup **butternut squash puree**
- ¼ cup firmly packed light brown sugar
- Juice of 1 lemon (about 2 tablespoons)
- 2 tablespoons whole-wheat flour
- 1 teaspoon ground cinnamon
- 1 teaspoon pure vanilla extract

TOPPING

- ½ cup walnuts, pecans, or almonds, roughly chopped
- 1 cup whole-wheat pastry flour
- 1¼ cups old-fashioned oats
- ¼ cup firmly packed light brown sugar
- 1 teaspoon ground cinnamon
- ¼ teaspoon salt
- ½ cup trans-fat-free soft tub margarine spread, frozen

1. Preheat the oven to 350°F. Coat a 9 x 13-inch baking dish with cooking spray. Peel, core, and slice the apples into ¼-inch slices. In a large mixing bowl, toss the apples, squash puree, brown sugar, lemon juice, flour, cinnamon, and vanilla. Transfer to the dish and spread out in an even layer. Set aside.

2. Make the topping. In another large bowl, mix together the nuts, pastry flour, oats, sugar, cinnamon, and salt. Using your fingertips, gently work in the frozen margarine until pea-size lumps form. If the margarine begins to melt, place the bowl in the freezer for 5 to 10 minutes.

3. Top the apples evenly with the nut mixture and bake, uncovered, until the apples are bubbly and the topping is golden brown, about 45 to 50 minutes. Serve warm or at room temperature.

Joy:
No problem getting kids to eat an "apple a day" when serving this homestyle dessert. Bonus—they'll get heart-healthy fats from the walnuts, fiber from the whole grains, and beta-carotene from the butternut squash.

Calories: 252, Carbohydrate: 35 g, Protein: 4 g, Total Fat: 11.5 g, Saturated Fat: 1.5 g, Sodium: 155 mg, Fiber: 5 g

Prep:
20 minutes

Total:
55 minutes

Yield:
Serves 8

Mixed Berry Cobbler

If you don't have fresh berries to make this wonderful dessert, frozen work just as well, and both are full of great antioxidants. Sprinkling boiling water over the whole-wheat topping makes it wonderfully crunchy.

- 4 cups assorted berries, such as strawberries, blueberries, or blackberries, fresh or, if frozen, thawed
- ½ cup **yellow squash** or **carrot puree**
- 2 tablespoons granulated sugar

TOPPING

- 1 cup white whole-wheat or whole-wheat pastry flour
- 6 tablespoons granulated sugar, divided
- 1 teaspoon baking powder
- ¼ teaspoon salt
- 3 tablespoons trans-fat-free soft tub margarine spread
- ½ cup low-fat (1%) buttermilk
- ½ teaspoon cinnamon
- 1 tablespoon cornstarch
- 1 cup boiling water

1. Preheat the oven to 350°F. Mix the berries, squash or carrot puree, and 2 tablespoons sugar in an 8 x 12-inch baking dish. Set aside.

2. Make the topping. Place the flour, 4 tablespoons of the sugar, baking powder, and salt in a food processor. Pulse 2 or 3 times to mix. Add the margarine and pulse 4 to 5 times, until the margarine forms pea-size balls with the flour. Do not overmix or the margarine will melt. Add the buttermilk and pulse 2 to 3 times, until the liquid begins to combine with the flour. (There might be some flour that is not mixed in, and the batter will be loose.) Do not overmix.

3. With a large spoon, dot the top of the berry mixture with the topping mixture.

4. In a medium bowl, stir the remaining 2 tablespoons of the sugar, cinnamon, and cornstarch. Sprinkle evenly over the topping mixture. Drizzle the boiling water over the cobbler and bake until the top is crispy and the topping is cooked through, 30 to 35 minutes.

With carrot puree:
Calories: 193, Carbohydrate: 36 g,
Protein: 3 g, Total Fat: 5 g, Saturated Fat: 0.5 g,
Sodium: 195 mg, Fiber: 5.5 g

With squash puree:
Calories: 190, Carbohydrate: 35 g,
Protein: 3 g, Total Fat: 5 g, Saturated Fat: 0.5 g,
Sodium: 185 mg, Fiber: 5 g

Tiramisu

This recipe is quick and fun, as well as being a no-bake dessert. Unlike traditional tiramisu recipes, it's not loaded with fat and has some bonus beta-carotene from the carrot!

QUICK!

Prep:
15 minutes

Total:
1 hour 15 minutes
(including chill time)

Yield:
Serves 8

CHOCOLATE FILLING
- ½ cup confectioners' sugar
- ½ cup **carrot puree**
- ½ cup fat-free sour cream
- 6 tablespoons unsweetened cocoa powder
- ½ cup warm water
- 1 tablespoon instant decaf coffee granules
- 1 tablespoon pure vanilla extract

RICOTTA FILLING
- 1 (15-ounce) container fat-free ricotta cheese
- 2 tablespoons reduced-fat sour cream
- 1 teaspoon pure vanilla extract
- ¼ cup confectioners' sugar
- 1 (3-ounce) package store-bought ladyfingers, or 3 ounces thinly sliced angel food cake
- ¼ teaspoon cinnamon
- ¼ cup chopped bittersweet chocolate

1. Make the chocolate filling. In a food processor, add the confectioners' sugar, carrot puree, sour cream, cocoa, water, coffee granules, and vanilla extract. Blend until smooth. Transfer to a bowl.

2. Make the cream filling. Rinse the food processor and add the ricotta, sour cream, vanilla extract, and confectioners' sugar. Blend until smooth.

3. Put ⅓ of the chocolate filling in a medium glass bowl. Press one-third of the ladyfingers or angel food cake over the chocolate. Top with ⅓ of the ricotta filling. Repeat, alternating layers of chocolate, ladyfingers or cake, and ricotta, ending with ricotta. Sprinkle with the cinnamon and chopped bittersweet chocolate. Cover and refrigerate. Chill at least 1 hour and serve.

Sascha:
The special hidden cookies are my favorite!

Calories: 194, Carbohydrate: 31 g, Protein: 9 g, Total Fat: 4.5 g, Saturated Fat: 2.5 g, Sodium: 175 mg, Fiber: 3 g

Nondairy Chocolate Pudding

Lots of people tell me they love the chocolate pudding in *Deceptively Delicious*, but I had some readers ask for a nondairy version. Here it is, friends—easy to make and delectable! (Dairy lovers will love it, too.)

Prep:
20 minutes

Total:
2 hours 20 minutes (including chill time)

Yield:
Serves 5

- 8 ounces silken tofu
- 1 cup light soy milk
- 1 packet unflavored gelatin
- 4 ounces semisweet chocolate chips
- 2 tablespoons honey

1. Place the tofu in a food processor and mix until smooth and creamy.

2. Bring the soy milk to a boil in a saucepan. Whisk in the gelatin.

3. In a medium bowl, pour the hot soy milk over the chocolate chips. Whisk to blend. Add the honey and whisk again.

4. Pour the tofu into the chocolate mixture and whisk until blended together.

5. Pour the mixture into a clean serving bowl and chill in the refrigerator for 2 hours.

Joy:
Tofu, the shining star in this recipe, provides protein, calcium, and iron, three nutrients that are vital for growing bodies.

Calories: 158, Carbohydrate: 22 g, Protein: 6 g, Total Fat: 7 g, Saturated Fat: 3 g, Sodium: 35 mg, Fiber: 2 g

Prep:
30 minutes

Total:
4 hours 50 minutes
(including chill time)

Yield:
Makes 24 tarts

Banana Chocolate Tarts

I don't know about you but I always have bananas in my house—and quite often they are turning brown. So I love using them to make this very simple dessert. The recipe couldn't be easier and my kids love making the dough into interesting shapes.

DOUGH

- ½ cup trans-fat-free soft tub margarine spread
- ¾ cup granulated sugar
- 2 large egg whites
- 2 teaspoons pure vanilla extract
- 1¼ cups whole-wheat pastry flour, plus ¼ cup to roll out the dough
- 1¼ cups all-purpose flour
- 1 teaspoon baking powder
- ¼ teaspoon salt
- ½ cup fat-free sour cream
- Nonstick cooking spray

FILLING

- 3 large ripe bananas, cut into ¼-inch-thick slices
- ½ cup bittersweet chocolate chips

1. To make the dough, place the margarine, sugar, egg whites, and vanilla in a large bowl and beat with an electric mixer on medium speed. Sprinkle both types of flour, the baking powder, and salt over the margarine mixture. On low speed, beat until small crumbs start to form, about 1 minute. Add the sour cream and mix on low speed until a soft dough forms.

2. Divide the dough into 2 equal portions. Shape each into a ball, then flatten into disks. Wrap in plastic wrap and refrigerate 3 to 4 hours or overnight. Let the dough soften slightly at room temperature before continuing.

3. Preheat the oven to 350°F. Coat 2 large baking sheets with cooking spray. On a work surface lightly sprinkled with the ¼ cup extra flour, roll out each disk into a ¼-inch-thick circle. Using a 2-inch round biscuit cutter or drinking glass, cut circles from the dough. Reroll the dough scraps and repeat.

(Continued on page 144)

1 serving = 1 tart
Calories: 151, Carbohydrate: 24 g, Protein: 2.5 g, Total Fat: 5.5 g, Saturated Fat: 1 g, Sodium: 95 mg, Fiber: 2 g

4. Transfer the tarts to the baking sheets and dot the center of each tart with 2 to 3 slices of banana and a ½ teaspoon of chocolate chips (about 3 to 4 chips) on one side of the circle. Fold the dough over and press the edges together with your fingertips.

5. Bake until the tarts are lightly browned and the dough is firm, 15 to 18 minutes.

6. Allow to cool completely on a wire rack before tasting—the filling will be hot. Cool completely before refrigerating in an airtight container for up to 3 days.

Julian:
Can I have a banana tart?

Jerry:
I finished them!

Jessica:
You finished all of them?

Other Mothers Know Best!

Toby, mother of Cleo (9) and Wilson (7):

I'm still surprised at how carrot and sweet potato "fries" get gobbled up the minute they're out of the oven. The thinner you cut them, the better—mix as many carrots and/or sweet potatoes as you can get on your roasting pan—but give them space. Spritz with cooking spray, sprinkle with sea or kosher salt, and roast in a preheated oven at 400°F for about 20 minutes, shoveling them around halfway through. They're done when they're carmelized and crispy-looking. I like making onion rings the same way—also sweet and tasty and good with any kind of meat.

Chocolate Peanut Butter Pie

This is the ultimate dessert! Peanut butter, graham crackers, and chocolate are all favorite treats in our house. If you are careful with your portion size, you can feel guilt-free about this healthier version of a beloved classic!

QUICK!

Prep:
20 minutes

Total:
2 hours 20 minutes
(including chill time)

Yield:
Serves 12

- 1½ cups reduced-fat honey graham cracker crumbs
- 3 tablespoons trans-fat-free soft tub margarine spread, melted
- 2 cups nonfat (skim) milk
- ¼ cup cornstarch
- ⅓ cup granulated sugar, plus 3 tablespoons
- ¼ teaspoon salt
- 1 large egg
- 1 large egg white
- 1 tablespoon pure vanilla extract
- ½ cup **yellow squash puree**
- ½ cup natural peanut butter (creamy)
- 1 tablespoon unsweetened cocoa powder
- 2 tablespoons shaved chocolate or chopped peanuts, for garnish (optional)

1. Preheat the oven to 350°F. In a medium bowl, combine the graham cracker crumbs and margarine. Pour into a 9-inch pie plate and press the crumb mixture into the bottom and sides of the plate to form an even crust. Bake for 5 minutes, or until golden brown. Set aside to cool.

2. In a large saucepan over medium heat, whisk together the milk, cornstarch, ⅓ cup of sugar, salt, egg, and egg white. Stir occasionally. When the mixture begins to thicken, stir constantly to avoid lumps. Turn off the heat when the mixture comes to a boil and has reached a pudding consistency.

3. Add the vanilla extract and squash puree. Pour half of the mixture into a medium bowl. Make the peanut butter layer by adding the remaining 3 tablespoons of sugar and peanut butter to one-half of the mixture and stirring to incorporate. Add the cocoa powder to the other half of the milk mixture to make the chocolate layer.

4. Pour the chocolate mixture into the pie crust, then top with the peanut butter layer. Cover with plastic wrap and refrigerate, at least 2 hours, until set. Garnish with shaved chocolate or peanuts.

Sascha:
My dad and I love to eat this together.

Calories: 219, Carbohydrate: 27 g, Protein: 6 g, Total Fat: 9.5 g, Saturated Fat: 1.5 g, Sodium: 225 mg, Fiber: 1 g

Prep:
25 minutes

Total:
40 minutes

Yield:
Makes 16 pies

Whoopie Pies

I had to include this family favorite. No, it is NOT APPROVED BY JOY BAUER. But it's very important that we all feel we can indulge (in moderation) once in a while. I cut these in half for my kids and we all share them.

CAKES

- 1 cup all-purpose flour
- 1 cup whole-wheat pastry flour
- ½ cup unsweetened cocoa powder
- 1 teaspoon baking soda
- ½ teaspoon baking powder
- ¼ teaspoon salt
- ½ cup light olive oil
- 1¼ cups packed brown sugar
- 2 egg whites
- ½ cup **spinach puree**
- 2 teaspoons pure vanilla extract
- ½ cup low-fat (1%) buttermilk
- Nonstick cooking spray

FILLING

- 1 stick (½ cup) unsalted butter, softened
- 1¼ cups confectioners' sugar
- 2 cups marshmallow cream
- 1 teaspoon pure vanilla extract

1. Preheat the oven to 350°F. Whisk together the flours, cocoa, baking soda, baking powder, and salt in a bowl or shake in a zipper-lock plastic bag until combined.

2. In a large bowl or standing mixer, beat the oil and brown sugar with an electric mixer at medium-high speed until well combined. Add the egg whites and mix on low until well blended. Blend in the spinach puree and vanilla.

3. Alternately add in the flour mixture and the buttermilk, beginning and ending with flour, mixing until smooth and just combined.

4. Coat 2 large baking sheets with cooking spray. Place tablespoonfuls of batter about 2 inches apart onto baking sheets. Bake until the cakes are cooked through and spring back to the touch, 8 to 10 minutes. Transfer to a rack to cool completely.

5. Make the filling. With an electric mixer on medium speed, beat together all the ingredients until smooth, about 3 minutes. Spread a rounded tablespoonful of filling on the flat sides of half of the cakes and top with the remaining cakes.

1 serving = 1 pie
Calories: 345, Carbohydrate: 55 g, Protein: 3 g, Total Fat: 13 g, Saturated Fat: 5 g, Sodium: 165 mg, Fiber: 2 g

Prep:
20 minutes

Total:
1 hour 10 minutes

Yield:
16 slices

Lemon Poppy Seed Cake

I love this cake with a nice hot cup of tea. My kids enjoy it with a glass of cold low-fat milk.

- Nonstick cooking spray
- ¾ cup granulated sugar
- ¼ cup reduced-fat cream cheese
- ⅓ cup light olive oil
- 2 large egg whites
- ½ cup **carrot puree**
- 1 tablespoon lemon zest
- ¼ cup lemon juice (from about 2 large lemons)
- 1 tablespoon poppy seeds
- 2 cups whole-wheat pastry flour or white whole-wheat flour
- ¼ cup flaxseed meal
- 2 teaspoons baking powder
- 1 teaspoon baking soda
- ¼ teaspoon salt

1. Coat a 1-pound loaf pan with cooking spray. Preheat the oven to 350°F.

2. In a large bowl, mash the sugar and cream cheese with a wooden spoon until well combined. Stir in the olive oil, egg whites, carrot puree, lemon zest, lemon juice, and poppy seeds. Mix well until smooth.

3. Add the flour, flaxseed meal, baking powder, baking soda, and salt. Stir until just combined—the batter will be slightly lumpy. Pour the dough into loaf pan and smooth the top with a rubber spatula.

4. Bake until the cake begins to brown around the edges and a toothpick comes out clean when inserted in the center, 45 to 50 minutes. Cool for five minutes in the pan. Transfer to a wire rack to cool completely.

Sascha:
I love lemon cake, lemon sorbet, lemonade, lemon cookies, lemon bars, lemon EVERYTHING!

1 serving = 1 slice
Calories: 158, Carbohydrate: 23 g, Protein: 3 g, Total Fat: 6 g, Saturated Fat: 1 g, Sodium: 170 mg, Fiber: 3 g

Cherries Jubilee Brownies

My husband is powerless to resist the chocolate-cherry combination and the cream cheese topping.

Prep:
20 minutes

Total:
1 hour

Yield:
Makes 12 brownies

- Nonstick cooking spray
- ¼ cup canola oil
- ⅔ cup bittersweet chocolate chips (4 ounces), melted
- ½ cup granulated sugar
- ½ cup **spinach puree**
- 2 large egg whites
- 2 teaspoons pure vanilla extract
- ⅔ cup all-purpose flour
- ½ teaspoon baking powder
- ¼ teaspoon salt
- 1 (10-ounce) bag "no sugar added" frozen cherries, defrosted, liquid drained (about 1½ cups cherries)

TOPPING
- 1/4 cup fat-free cream cheese
- 1 tablespoon all-purpose flour
- 1 tablespoon confectioners' sugar
- 1 large egg white
- 1 teaspoon pure vanilla extract

1. Preheat the oven to 350°F. Coat an 8 x 8-inch baking pan with cooking spray. In a large bowl, combine the oil, chocolate chips, sugar, spinach puree, egg whites, and vanilla. Blend until smooth. Add the flour, baking powder, and salt. Blend on low speed, 1 to 2 minutes, until smooth. Stir in the cherries. Transfer the batter to the pan and smooth with a rubber spatula.

2. Make the topping. In a separate bowl, blend the cream cheese, flour, and confectioners' sugar. Add the egg white and vanilla, and mix until creamy.

3. Dot the cream cheese mixture on top of the batter. Run a toothpick through the cream cheese mixture to make swirls. Bake until the edges of the brownie are firm but the center is still soft, 35 to 40 minutes. Cool completely in the pan and then cut into 12 squares.

1 serving = 1 brownie
Calories: 184, Carbohydrate: 25 g, Protein: 3.5 g, Total Fat: 8.5 g, Saturated Fat: 2.5 g, Sodium: 110 mg, Fiber: 1.5 g

Prep:
10 minutes

Total:
30 minutes

Yield:
Makes 48 cookies

Cinnamon Raisin Peanut Butter Cookies

This combination of flavors is so delicious, so fragrant, just perfect.

- 2 cups whole-wheat pastry flour
- 1 teaspoon baking soda
- 1 teaspoon cinnamon
- ½ teaspoon kosher salt
- 1 cup natural peanut butter (creamy)
- ¾ cup pure maple syrup
- ½ cup **carrot puree**
- ¼ cup canola oil
- 2 teaspoons pure vanilla extract
- ½ cup raisins
- Nonstick cooking spray

1. Preheat the oven to 350°F. In a mixing bowl, combine the flour, baking soda, cinnamon, and salt. Set aside.

2. In a large bowl, mix together the peanut butter, maple syrup, carrot puree, canola oil, and vanilla. Stir until combined.

3. Pour the flour mixture over the peanut butter mixture. Turn the batter over with a spatula about 7 times. Do not overmix! There will be dry spots. Stir in raisins.

4. While the batter is resting, spray 2 baking sheets with cooking spray. Using a 2-ounce ice cream scoop, drop tablespoonfuls of dough onto the baking sheets 1 inch apart. Fill a small bowl with water and, using a fork, press down on the dough, making a crisscross on each cookie. Wet the fork each time.

5. Bake for 8 to 10 minutes. Transfer the cookies to a wire rack to cool before packing in an airtight container for up to 4 days.

Jerry:
If these are left out at night, it is highly unlikely there will be any left in the morning.

1 serving = 2 cookies
Calories: 166, Carbohydrate: 20 g, Protein: 4 g, Total Fat: 8 g, Saturated Fat: 1 g, Sodium: 135 mg, Fiber: 2.5 g

Prep:
30 minutes

Total:
40 minutes

Yield:
Makes 20 cookies

Chocolate Chip Cookies

I heard a lot of enthusiasm for the chocolate chip cookies in Deceptively Delicious. So I developed this version, which adds the benefits of whole grains.

- 1 (15-ounce) can low-sodium chickpeas, drained and rinsed
- Nonstick cooking spray
- 1½ cups white whole-wheat flour
- ½ teaspoon baking soda
- ¼ teaspoon salt
- 6 tablespoons trans-fat-free soft tub margarine spread
- ¼ cup granulated sugar
- ½ cup firmly packed light brown sugar
- ¼ cup unsweetened applesauce
- 2 tablespoons nonfat (skim) milk
- 1 tablespoon pure vanilla extract
- 2 large egg whites
- ½ cup semisweet chocolate chips

1. In a mini-chopper, puree the chickpeas until smooth, then set aside. Preheat the oven to 375°F. Coat 2 large baking sheets with cooking spray.

2. In large bowl, mix the flour, baking soda, and salt. Set aside.

3. In another large bowl, beat the margarine, sugars, and applesauce with an electric mixer on low speed for 1 to 2 minutes until smooth. Add the chickpeas, milk, vanilla extract, and egg whites. Blend until smooth. Slowly add the dry ingredients and chocolate chips, and mix with a spatula until the flour is just combined.

4. With a 2-ounce ice cream scoop, drop the dough onto the baking sheets and space each scoop 1 inch apart. Bake until the cookies are golden brown, about 10 to 12 minutes. Cool on the baking sheets 1 to 2 minutes before transferring the cookies to a wire rack to cool completely.

Jessica:
I make these large so that you only eat one, but one is enough because they are very satisfying.

1 serving = 1 cookie
Calories: 135, Carbohydrate: 20 g, Protein: 3 g, Total Fat: 5 g, Saturated Fat: 1 g, Sodium: 135 mg, Fiber: 2.5 g

Prep:
30 minutes

Total:
1 hour

Yield:
Makes 50 cookies

Doughnut Cookies

Crafting doughnuts is a perfect holiday baking activity. The two glazes—lemon and chocolate—are so simple to make and kids love to drizzle them on the cookies themselves.

Doughnut Cookies shown with Lemon Cream Cookies (recipe page 161).

- Nonstick cooking spray
- 2 cups whole-wheat pastry flour or white whole-wheat flour
- ¼ cup granulated sugar
- 1 teaspoon baking powder
- ¼ cup light olive oil
- 2 large eggs
- 1 teaspoon pure almond or vanilla extract

CHOCOLATE GLAZE

- 2 teaspoons unsweetened cocoa powder
- 1¼ tablespoons confectioners' sugar
- 1 tablespoon nonfat (skim) milk
- 1 teaspoon pure vanilla extract

LEMON GLAZE

- 2 tablespoons confectioners' sugar
- 2 teaspoons fresh lemon juice, from ½ lemon
- ½ teaspoon grated lemon zest, from ½ lemon

1. Preheat the oven to 350° F. Coat 2 large baking sheets with cooking spray. In a large bowl, mix the flour, sugar, and baking powder.

2. Make a well in the center of the flour with a wooden spoon. Place the oil, eggs, and almond or vanilla extract in the well. Mix the liquid while incorporating the flour. When most of the flour is absorbed and the dough is firm and no longer sticky, turn it out onto a lightly floured surface.

3. Bring the dough together into a ball. Knead by pressing the dough down onto the surface away from you, gathering the drier crumbs as you continue. Knead the dough 12 to 15 times, until it no longer sticks to your fingers and no dry spots remain.

(Continued on page 160)

Jessica:
Kneading the dough helps to release the gluten to make it more elastic and easy to handle.

---

1 serving = 2 cookies
For chocolate or lemon glaze:
Calories: 70, Carbohydrate: 10 g, Protein: 1.5 g, Total Fat: 2.5 g, Saturated Fat: 0.5 g, Sodium: 15 mg, Fiber: 1.5 g

4. Roll 1 teaspoonful of dough between your fingers and squeeze the ends together to form a doughnut. Place on a baking sheet and repeat with the remaining dough, spacing them about ½-inch apart. You'll have about 50 mini doughnut cookies. Bake 5 to 8 minutes until the doughnuts are firm but not hard. Transfer to a wire rack to cool completely.

5. To prepare the chocolate or lemon glaze, mix all the ingredients for each glaze with a teaspoon in a small bowl until smooth. Once the doughnut cookies are cool, dip the tops into the glaze. Place on a sheet of waxed paper until the glaze dries, about 20 minutes. Store in an airtight container for up to 3 days.

Shepherd:
I like the chocolate.

Sascha:
I like the lemon.

Julian:
I like them both!

Joy:
These mini cookies are just enough to satisfy your little one's sweet tooth—without going overboard on dessert. Serve them with a cold glass of skim milk.

Lemon Cream Cookies

Hands down, the best cookie I have ever tasted. Our family, and all of our friends, go insane for these. In fact, one friend told me she was "possessed" by them. Photograph page 159.

Prep:
30 minutes

Total:
1 hour 50 minutes
(including chill time)

Yield:
Makes 50 cookies

- Nonstick cooking spray

FILLING

- 2 tablespoons reduced-fat cream cheese, at room temperature
- 2 tablespoons confectioners' sugar
- 2 tablespoons **yellow squash puree**
- Zest of 1 lemon (about 1 teaspoon)
- 1 teaspoon pure lemon extract

COOKIES

- 1¼ cups whole-wheat pastry flour
- ¼ cup flaxseed meal
- 1 teaspoon baking soda
- ¼ teaspoon salt
- ¾ cup trans-fat-free soft tub margarine spread
- 1 cup granulated sugar
- 1 tablespoon lemon zest
- 1 teaspoon lemon juice

1. Coat 3 baking sheets with cooking spray. Make the filling. In a large bowl, beat the cream cheese and confectioners' sugar with an electric mixer until smooth and creamy. Beat in the squash puree, lemon zest, and extract. Refrigerate.

2. Make the cookies. In a large bowl mix the flour, flaxseed meal, baking soda, and salt until well combined. In a separate bowl, mix the margarine, sugar, zest, and juice with a wooden spoon until just combined. Stir in the flour mixture. Divide the dough into 3 pieces and shape into disks. Wrap in plastic wrap and refrigerate for 1 hour.

3. Roll out each disk between plastic wrap. Cut with a 2-inch cookie cutter. Transfer to the baking sheets. Repeat with the remaining dough.

4. Bake until the cookies begin to brown around the edges and become firm to the touch, 7 to 10 minutes. Leave on the baking sheets for 5 minutes before transferring to a wire rack to cool completely.

5. Spread ½ teaspoon of the filling on half the cookies. Top with the remaining cookies.

1 serving = 2 cookies
Calories: 113, Carbohydrate: 14 g, Protein: 1 g, Total Fat: 6 g, Saturated Fat: 1 g, Sodium: 150 mg, Fiber: 1 g

Lemon Bars

The Seinfelds love lemon, specifically these lemon bars. The whole-grain crust is a healthy twist on the classic recipe, as is the low-fat topping. But they still have the same luscious flavor as the full-fat version, I'm happy to report.

Prep:
30 minutes

Total:
1 hour 45 minutes

Yield:
Makes 12 bars

CRUST
- Nonstick cooking spray
- ½ cup whole-wheat pastry flour
- 2 tablespoons flaxseed meal
- 1 tablespoon granulated sugar
- Pinch of salt
- Pinch of ground cinnamon
- 3 tablespoons trans-fat-free soft-tub margarine spread, frozen

FILLING
- ¾ cup granulated sugar
- ¼ cup whole-wheat flour
- ¼ teaspoon salt
- 1 tablespoon plus 2 teaspoons finely grated lemon zest
- 2 teaspoons finely grated orange zest
- 5 large eggs
- 1 cup fresh lemon juice
- ½ cup **cauliflower puree**
- ½ cup nonfat (skim) milk
- 2¼ tablespoons cornstarch
- 2 teaspoons confectioners' sugar for dusting (optional)

1. Preheat the oven to 350°F. Lightly spray an 8 x 12-inch ceramic or glass baking dish. In a food processor, combine the flour, flaxseed meal, granulated sugar, salt, and cinnamon. Pulse briefly until blended. Add the margarine and pulse about 8 to 10 times, until the dough forms moist crumbs and sticks together when pressed. The dough should look crumbly. Do not overwork—otherwise the crust will be tough.

2. Press the dough into the bottom of the prepared baking dish, using a rubber spatula and not your fingers. Bake the crust until pale golden, 20 to 25 minutes. Transfer the pan to a wire rack and let the crust cool completely. Reduce the oven temperature to 325°F.

3. To make the filling, whisk together the sugar, flour, salt, lemon and orange zest in a large bowl. Add the eggs, lemon juice, cauliflower puree, milk, and cornstarch. Carefully pour the mixture over the baked crust. Bake until the filling is set but still jiggles slightly when the dish is gently shaken, about 35 to 40 minutes. *(Continued on page 164)*

---

1 serving = 1 bar
(including confectioners' sugar for dusting)
Calories: 157, Carbohydrate: 24 g, Protein: 4 g, Total Fat: 5 g, Saturated Fat: 1 g, Sodium: 140 mg, Fiber: 2 g

4. Transfer the dish to the wire rack and let cool for about 30 minutes. Run the tip of a small knife along the inside of the dish to loosen the bars from the sides of the pan, then cool completely.

5. Cut into 12 small rectangles. Using a spatula, carefully remove the bars from the dish. Just before serving, sift a dusting of confectioners' sugar over the bars, if desired.

ZEST IT UP!

*L*emon, lime, or orange zest is a wonderful way to add instant flavor to anything from cookies to soups to salads without adding calories, fat, sodium, or sugar. The oils in the rind pass on a gorgeous, fresh flavor.

The best tool to get long, threadlike strands is a zester. But you can use a cheese grater, paring knife, or vegetable peeler and finely chop the peel. Just make sure you get only the zest and as little of the bitter white pith as possible. If you can, choose organic fruit that hasn't been treated with dye or wax.

Other Mothers Know Best!

Orli, mother of Scarlet (5) and Kate (7):

Whole-wheat couscous is one of my standbys. It's a mild-flavored source of good whole grains that everyone likes, and it takes no effort to prepare. Just boil water, throw in the couscous, remove from the heat, and let steep for a few minutes until the water is absorbed. It's that easy. It makes a great side dish, or is perfect with a little tomato sauce or steamed veggies on top. My kids eat it cold for lunch the next day with raisins, chopped apple, and a sprinkling of toasted nuts.

I got my kids to eat quinoa by lightly toasting it before cooking. Just a few moments in a dry skillet gives it a wonderfully nutty flavor they really love. Works with barley, too.

Prep:
20 minutes

Total:
50 minutes

Yield:
Makes 48 cookies

Blythe's Thumbprint Cookies

This is a lovely nondairy/wheat-free dessert recipe given to me by my friend's mother. They take no time to prepare and bake.

Shown here with Ginger Cookies and Fig Bars (recipes pages 168 and 169).

- ½ cup ground almonds
- 1½ cups barley flour
- ½ cup pure maple syrup
- ½ cup canola oil
- 1 teaspoon pure vanilla extract
- ¼ teaspoon salt
- ½ cup strawberry, apricot, or any fruit jam
- Nonstick cooking spray

1. Preheat the oven to 350°F. Place the almonds, barley flour, maple syrup, canola oil, vanilla, and salt in a large bowl. Beat on low speed until well combined and then mix on high for 30 seconds until texture becomes fluffy.

2. Coat 2 large baking sheets with nonstick spray. Drop 12 tablespoonfuls of dough, 1 inch apart, onto each baking sheet. Press the center of each cookie with your thumb. Fill each cookie with ½ teaspoonful of jam.

3. Bake until the edges are lightly browned, 10 to 15 minutes. Repeat with the remaining dough. Transfer to a wire rack to cool completely. Store in an airtight container for up to 3 days.

Jessica:
I make these cookies really small because I find they are crispier and the kids think they are very cute that way.

1 serving = 2 cookies
Calories: 120, Carbohydrate: 16 g, Protein 1.5 g, Total Fat: 6 g, Saturated Fat: 0 g, Sodium: 25 mg, Fiber: 1 g

Prep:
20 minutes

Total:
40 minutes

Yield:
Makes 60 cookies

Ginger Cookies

I love how soft and sweet these cookies are! Fall and winter are the usual seasons for Ginger Cookies, but I make them year-round.

Photograph page 167.

- 1 cup whole-wheat flour
- 1¼ cups all-purpose flour
- 4 teaspoons allspice
- 4 teaspoons ground ginger
- 2 teaspoons cinnamon
- ½ teaspoon salt
- 1½ teaspoons baking soda
- 1 cup granulated sugar
- ¾ cup canola oil
- ½ cup **pureed pumpkin** (solid-pack pumpkin in a can), at room temperature
- 1 large egg
- 1 teaspoon pure vanilla extract
- ⅓ cup molasses
- 1 cup canned black beans, rinsed and pureed

1. Preheat the oven to 350°F. In a small bowl, mix together both types of flour, the spices, salt, and baking soda.

2. In a large mixing bowl, beat the sugar, canola oil, pumpkin, egg, and vanilla until smooth and fluffy. Add the molasses and beans. Stir well. Slowly add the dry ingredients to form a smooth, soft dough.

3. Drop teaspoonfuls of dough onto a lightly greased baking sheet. Bake for 10 to 12 minutes. Do not overbake! Cool on wire racks.

Jessica:
I like to undercook these just a bit so that they stay soft and moist inside.

Shepherd:
I love when they are warm in the middle.

1 serving = 2 cookies
Calories: 128, Carbohydrate: 18 g, Protein: 2 g, Total Fat: 6 g, Saturated Fat: 0.5 g, Sodium: 120 mg, Fiber: 1.5 g

Fig Bars

No one believes me when I tell them what is stashed inside—
a nice, healthy portion of spinach, which is totally undetectable.
My kids marvel at how similar mine look to the store-bought kind.

Photograph page 167.

Prep:
30 minutes

Total:
45 minutes (plus
overnight chilling)

Yield:
Makes 20 cookies

- 1 cup whole-wheat pastry flour
- 1 cup all-purpose flour
- ¼ teaspoon baking soda
- ⅛ teaspoon baking powder
- ⅛ teaspoon salt
- 3 teaspoons canola oil
- 1½ tablespoons honey
- 3–4 tablespoons water
- 2 large egg whites
- 2 tablespoons lemon juice
- Nonstick cooking spray

    FILLING
- 1 pound dried figs
- ½ cup water
- 2 tablespoons 100% orange juice
  concentrate
- 2 tablespoons honey
- ¾ cup **spinach puree**
- Nonstick cooking spray

1. In a large bowl, mix the flours, baking soda, baking powder, and salt with a wooden spoon. Make a well in the center of the flour mixture and add the oil, honey, 2 tablespoons water, egg whites, and lemon juice. Mix well until a smooth dough forms. Add 1 to 2 tablespoons more water if the dough is too dry. Wrap tightly in plastic wrap and refrigerate the dough overnight.

2. Make the filling. Chop the figs in a food processor with ½ cup of water. Spoon the puree into a medium saucepan and add the orange concentrate and honey. Bring the mixture to a boil, then lower the heat to medium. Cook until most of the liquid evaporates and the mixture is thick, stirring occasionally, about 4 to 5 minutes. Remove from the heat. Stir in the spinach puree. If the mixture is not smooth, return it to the food processor and process for 30 seconds.

(Continued on page 170)

1 serving = 1 bar
Calories: 127, Carbohydrate: 28 g, Protein: 3 g, Total Fat: 1 g, Saturated Fat: 0 g, Sodium: 45 mg, Fiber: 3.5 g

3. Preheat the oven to 325°F. Coat a baking sheet with cooking spray. Remove the dough from the refrigerator and divide it into 4 equal parts. Roll each part out into a rectangle about ¼ inch thick. Spread the filling equally over each section of the dough. Fold both long sides towards the middle, overlapping them to form a seam. Place the rolls seam-side down onto the baking sheet.

4. Bake until the rolls brown slightly and are firm to the touch, 12 to 15 minutes. Cool for 5 minutes, then cut each roll into 5 cookies. Once cooled, store in an airtight container for up to 3 days.

Joy:
Dried figs are a fabulous source of fiber, potassium, and iron.

Other Mothers Know Best!

Amy, mother of Finn (7) and Ada (4):

Usually my son will eat an entire sliced apple with each meal. Our daughter will
eat an orange. After they finish their fruit, I give them small portions of veggies such
as steamed broccoli, baby carrots, and edamame, each on its own very small dish.
There is the miniature aspect, which the kids really like. Then, once they are
close to finishing their tiny plates of veggies, I offer them a small bowl
of rice and a protein, like stir-fried chicken, beef, pork, or tofu.

Mary Ellen, mother of Kate (12):

I hate buying creamy store-bought dips, which can be high in fat and sodium. Instead,
I puree some canned beans with a little garlic, chopped tomato, and finely chopped onion
or scallions as a dip for tortilla chips or sliced raw veggies.

Prep:
15 minutes

Total:
45 minutes

Yield:
Makes 48 cookies

Oatmeal Raisin Cookies

They've been around forever, but this is a new and nutritious take on a classic.

- Nonstick cooking spray
- 1½ cups old-fashioned oats
- 1 cup whole-wheat pastry flour or white whole-wheat flour
- ½ cup raisins
- ½ teaspoon baking powder
- 1 teaspoon ground cinnamon
- ½ teaspoon nutmeg
- ¼ teaspoon salt
- 6 tablespoons canola oil
- ½ cup firmly packed light brown sugar
- ½ cup **sweet potato puree**
- 2 large egg whites
- 2 teaspoons pure vanilla extract
- ⅓ cup bittersweet chocolate chips

1. Preheat the oven to 350°F. Coat 2 large baking sheets with cooking spray.

2. In a large bowl, mix the oats, flour, raisins, baking powder, cinnamon, nutmeg, and salt. Set aside.

3. In another large bowl, using a wooden spoon, mix the oil into the brown sugar until well combined. Mix in the sweet potato puree, egg whites, and vanilla. Add the chocolate chips.

4. Add the flour mixture all at once. Stir until a thick dough forms. Drop the dough by the tablespoonful about 1 inch apart onto the prepared baking sheets. Flatten the cookie mounds with the back of a fork.

5. Bake the cookies until they are golden brown around the edges, about 12 to 15 minutes. Using a metal spatula, move the cookies onto a rack and let them cool completely. Repeat with the rest of the cookies.

1 serving = 2 cookies
Calories: 114, Carbohydrate: 17 g, Protein: 2 g, Total Fat: 5 g, Saturated Fat: 1 g, Sodium: 35 mg, Fiber: 1.5 g

Cranberry Biscotti

I like to have these biscotti around because they're low in fat and calories and are such a nice treat when friends come over for tea or coffee. This version is made with whole grains.

Shown here with Chocolate Biscotti (recipe page 176).

Prep:
20 minutes

Total:
1 hour

Yield:
Makes 40 cookies

- 1½ cups oat flour
- 2⅓ cups whole-wheat pastry flour, plus 2 tablespoons for rolling out
- 2½ teaspoons baking soda
- ¼ teaspoon baking powder
- ¼ teaspoon salt
- ¼ cup canola oil
- 1¼ cups granulated sugar
- 2 large eggs
- 2 large egg whites
- Zest of 1 lemon (about 2 teaspoons)
- Zest of 1 orange (about 1 tablespoon)
- ⅓ cup unsweetened applesauce
- 1 teaspoon pure almond extract
- 1½ teaspoons pure vanilla extract
- ½ cup dried cranberries
- Nonstick cooking spray

1. Preheat the oven to 375°F. In a large bowl or zipper-lock plastic bag, mix the flours, baking soda, baking powder, and salt. In another large bowl mix the oil, sugar, eggs, egg whites, zests, applesauce, and extracts on low speed until smooth. Gradually add the flour mixture and mix until a smooth, soft dough forms. Stir in the cranberries.

2. Coat 3 baking sheets with nonstick cooking spray. Cut the dough in thirds. With floured hands, transfer each section of dough onto separate baking sheets. Form into two 10-inch logs.

3. Bake until the logs are firm to the touch, 15 to 20 minutes. Remove the logs from the baking sheets and, using a serrated knife, cut into ½-inch-thick slices. Return to the baking sheets, cut-side down, and bake 20 to 25 minutes more, until the cookies are crisp. Transfer to a wire rack to cool completely.

1 serving = 1 cookie
Calories: 86, Carbohydrate: 15.5 g, Protein: 1.5 g, Total Fat: 2 g, Saturated Fat: 0 g, Sodium: 100 mg, Fiber: 1.5 g

Prep:
30 minutes

Total:
2½ hours

Yield:
Makes 40 cookies

Chocolate Biscotti

Chocolate and almonds are a match made in heaven! For so little chocolate these biscotti have a very rich, satisfying flavor.

Photograph page 174.

- Nonstick cooking spray
- 1 cup all-purpose flour
- 1 cup whole-wheat pastry flour or white whole-wheat flour
- ½ cup unsweetened cocoa powder
- 1 teaspoon baking soda
- ¼ teaspoon salt
- ¾ cup firmly packed dark brown sugar
- ¼ cup **carrot puree**
- 1 large egg
- 2 large egg whites
- 2 teaspoons pure vanilla extract
- 2 teaspoons pure almond extract
- ½ cup slivered almonds
- ¼ cup bittersweet chocolate chips

TOPPING

- ¼ cup bittersweet chocolate chips
- 1 tablespoon trans-fat-free soft tub margarine spread

1. Preheat the oven to 300°F. Coat 2 large baking sheets with cooking spray. Set aside. Sift together both types of flour, cocoa powder, baking soda, and salt into a bowl. Set aside. In a large bowl, beat the sugar, carrot puree, egg, egg whites, and vanilla and almond extracts with an electric mixer on medium speed until smooth.

2. Reduce the speed to low and mix in the flour mixture until a soft dough forms, adding the almonds and chocolate chips when the dough is about half mixed.

3. On a floured surface, divide the dough in half. Form each half into a log 12 inches long. Transfer the logs to a prepared baking sheet, spacing them well apart, and pat to even the shapes.

4. Bake until almost firm to the touch, about 50 minutes—logs will spread during baking. Remove from the oven and let cool for 10 minutes. Leave the oven set at 300°F.

1 serving = 1 cookie
Calories: 70, Carbohydrate: 11 g, Protein: 1.5 g, Total Fat: 2.5 g, Saturated Fat: 1 g, Sodium: 55 mg, Fiber: 1 g

5. Using a spatula, carefully transfer the logs to a work surface. Using a serrated knife, cut logs on the diagonal into slices ½ to ¾ inch thick. Arrange the slices, cut-side down, on the baking sheets. Bake for 45 to 50 minutes more, until crisp, turning once. Transfer to a wire rack to cool completely.

6. Make the topping. Place chocolate chips in a small glass bowl with the margarine. Microwave on high for 40 to 50 seconds until the chocolate is melted. Stir well. Top each cookie with a teaspoonful of the chocolate mixture and smooth with a spoon.

Joy:
Using cocoa and bittersweet chocolate (instead of milk chocolate) gives these treats a little antioxidant boost, thanks to their high concentration of plant compounds called flavonoids.

Prep:
15 minutes

Total:
1 hour 15 minutes
(including chill time)

Yield:
8 banana pops

Frozen Banana Pops

Anyone can make these—no cooking skills required! This is such a fun activity to do with your kids.

- 8 wooden ice-pop sticks or 4-inch wooden skewers
- 4 bananas, peeled and halved
- ⅓ cup bittersweet chocolate chips
- 4 teaspoons trans-fat-free soft tub margarine spread
- ¼ cup unsweetened shredded coconut
- ¼ cup crushed whole-grain cereal, such as whole-grain crisped rice (optional)
- 2 tablespoons flaxseed meal

1. Insert an ice-pop stick or wooden skewer into the flat end of each banana. Place the chocolate chips and margarine in a glass 1-cup measuring cup. Microwave 40 to 50 seconds on high, uncovered, until the margarine is melted and the chips are completely melted. Stir to combine the chocolate and margarine.

2. Mix the coconut, cereal, and flaxseed meal on waxed paper with your fingertips. Dip the bananas into the melted chocolate. Immediately roll in coconut topping. Place the bananas on a 12 x 16-inch sheet of waxed paper.

3. Once all the bananas are dipped, fold the waxed paper in half to cover and wrap in aluminum foil. Freeze until solid, about 1 hour, before serving. These keep up to 2 months in the freezer in an airtight container.

Shepherd:
I like mine crunchy with brown rice cereal!

Julian:
I'm rolling mine in coconut.

1 serving = 1 pop (1/2 banana)
Calories: 139, Carbohydrate: 19 g, Protein: 2 g, Total Fat: 7.5 g, Saturated Fat: 3.5 g, Sodium: 25 mg, Fiber: 3 g

Carrot Orange Pops

When I make fresh-squeezed orange juice it turns sour after a couple of days. That's why I came up with this recipe—to use up the extra and freeze it while the nutrients are still at their best.

QUICK!

Prep:
5 minutes

Total:
2 hours 5 minutes
(including chill time)

Yield:
Makes 6 ice pops

- 1½ cups 100% orange juice
- ½ cup **carrot puree**
- 1 ice-pop mold
- 6 wooden ice-pop sticks

1. Whisk the orange juice and the carrot puree until smooth. Divide the liquid between the ice-pop molds. Insert the ice-pop sticks or handles.

2. Freeze at least 2 hours until firm.

Sascha:
I can make these all by myself.

Julian:
I like to help.

1 serving = 1 pop
Calories: 39, Carbohydrate: 9 g, Protein: 1 g, Total Fat: 0 g, Saturated Fat: 0 g, Sodium: 19 mg, Fiber: 1 g

Mint Chocolate Chip Ice Cream

It's astonishing that such a special treat can be made so easily! You can whip up this refreshing dessert in no time at all.

QUICK!

Prep:
10 minutes

Total:
2 hours 10 minutes
(including chill time)

Yield:
Serves 12

- ½ cup **spinach puree**
- ¼ teaspoon pure mint extract
- 3 cups nonfat plain Greek yogurt
- 1 cup confectioners' sugar
- 1 cup bittersweet chocolate chips

1. Place the spinach puree and mint extract in a mini-chopper and puree until very smooth.

2. In a medium bowl, stir the spinach mixture, yogurt, confectioners' sugar, and chocolate chips. Freeze in an airtight container at least 2 hours until solid.

Jessica:
The key to this recipe is very smooth spinach puree.

Kids:
There is spinach in here? WOW! You can't tell!

Calories: 147, Carbohydrate: 20g, Protein: 6 g, Total Fat: 6 g, Saturated Fat: 3 g, Sodium: 25 mg, Fiber: 1 g

Caramel Corn

We make this really special, easy-to-prepare treat for movie night at our house. Because of the sugar, I'm careful with the portion size and make little bowls for everyone.

Prep:
25 minutes

Total:
1 hour

Yield:
Serves 12

- 1¼ cups popcorn kernels
- 1 teaspoon canola oil
- ¼ cup firmly packed light brown sugar
- ¼ cup honey
- ¾ cup **sweet potato puree**
- ¼ cup flaxseed meal
- ¼ teaspoon salt
- Nonstick cooking spray

Jessica:
*To watch the sugar intake,
I combine the caramel corn with
plain popped popcorn.*

1. In a medium saucepan over medium-high heat, combine the popcorn and canola oil. Cover and let cook, shaking the pot occasionally, until you hear the popcorn begin to pop, approximately 1 to 2 minutes. Once the popcorn begins to pop, shake the pot continuously until the popping slows down to once every few seconds. Turn off the heat and leave the pot covered until all the popping has stopped. Transfer the popcorn to a large bowl.

2. Preheat the oven to 350°F. In a small, heavy-bottomed saucepan, combine the brown sugar and honey. Over medium heat, bring to a boil and cook 2 to 3 minutes, taking care not to burn the sugar mixture. Whisk in the sweet potato puree, flaxseed meal, and salt.

3. Pour the mixture over the popcorn and toss to evenly coat the kernels. Spread the mixture onto two large rimmed baking sheets sprayed with cooking spray.

4. Bake for 40 minutes. Stir occasionally at the beginning and more frequently as the mixture begins to dry out. The mixture will be soggy at first but after it cools, it will be crisp and delicious! Store in a zipper-lock plastic bag.

Calories: 133, Carbohydrate: 30 g, Protein: 3 g, Total Fat: 2 g, Saturated Fat: 0 g, Sodium: 60 mg, Fiber: 4.5 g

Prep:
10 minutes

Total:
10 minutes

Yield:
Serves 5

Watermelon Punch

Simply the most refreshing drink I have ever tasted! Serve on a hot summer's day at a barbecue or picnic. Or keep an ice-cold pitcher of it in the fridge all summer long.

Photograph page 116.

- 5 cups cubed, seeded watermelon
- 1 cup water
- ½ cup **carrot puree**
- 1 tablespoon granulated sugar
- ½ teaspoon cinnamon

1. Combine all the ingredients in a blender or food processor. Blend until smooth, then chill or serve over ice.

Sascha:
*We love this special Watermelon Punch.
Shepherd thinks it's a little spicy
but it's just cinnamon.*

Calories: 70, Carbohydrate: 17 g, Protein: 1 g, Total Fat: 0 g, Saturated Fat: 0 g, Sodium: 25 mg, Fiber: 1.5 g

Essentials

Equipment

I received so many e-mails, letters, and comments from Deceptively Delicious readers who loved my primer on kitchen basics that I've decided to bring them back for this book, too—so that they are always at your fingertips. Of course, I've learned a few new tips since then, so consider this a new and improved kitchen update! The tools for pureeing remain the must-have items for my kitchen. What works best, however, is a matter of personal choice.

I've heard from a lot of home cooks that when it comes to puree-ing, size does matter. When you are attacking a big batch of vegetables or fruit, many of you like the power of a standard-sized food processor or blender. For me, counter space and sink space are an issue, so I am still partial to a mini-food processor, because I can make small batches on the fly. But I often find myself using the standard size processor to make big batches of purees.

For steaming, the choices are the old standards: a collapsible steamer, pasta pot with a drainer basket, or rice steamer. I use them all, depending on what I'm steaming and how much, but for convenience, nothing beats my rice steamer, simply because if I get distracted (or more likely, if my kids distract me), the steamer is on a timer and turns off automatically, keeping everything warm. In my life, and I'm guessing in yours, it's all about multitasking.

FOR
Pureeing

- Blender, food processor, or immersion blender
- Rice steamer, collapsible steamer, or pasta pot with a drainer basket
- Strainer or colander
- Cutting board
- Vegetable peeler
- Large (10-inch) chef's knife
- Small paring knife
- 1- and 2-quart saucepans
- 6- and 8-quart pots

- Kitchen timer
- Wooden spoons: small, medium, large
- Measuring cups and spoons
- Food storage bags
- Black permanent markers to label puree bags
- Optional: ice cube trays or muffin tins for purees

HELPFUL
Tools

- Plastic storage bins
- Scissors (to snip open zipper-lock plastic bags of puree)
- Box grater
- Waxed paper, aluminum foil, and cooking parchment
- Potato ricer or potato masher
- Large (12-inch) nonstick skillet and large ovenproof nonstick skillet

- Baking dishes
- Ice-pop mold (2-ounce pops)
- 9 x 5-inch loaf pan
- Immersion blender
- Citrus zester or grater

FOR
Baking

- Heatproof silicone spatula
- Whisk
- Mixing bowls
- Ice cream scoop for filling muffin cups
- 12-cup and 6-cup muffin pan
- Large baking sheets
- Baking pans (8 x 8-inch and 9 x 12-inch)

- Cooling rack
- 9-inch cake pan
- 9-inch pie plate
- Electric mixer (optional, but great to have)
- Paper baking cups

The Purees: How To

I'm committed, as always, to the virtues of purees. So here's a refresher course on the A–B–Cs of what I think is one of the most beneficial parts of my recipes.

If you are brand-new to pureeing and don't know what will work best for your family, I recommend starting with nongreen veggies—cauliflower, butternut squash, sweet potato, carrots, zucchini, and yellow squash. They are harder to see, and many people feel they don't have as distinctive a taste either. Start with a pound of each veggie or a head of cauliflower.

As before, I do still try to make all my purees for the week in one kitchen session. You can do this even without a meal plan—just keep a healthy stock of all purees in your freezer at all times. I'll say it again: It takes only an hour to make a ton of purees, and it's such easy work that you can do other things while you are pureeing—pay some bills, answer e-mails, or catch up with your friends or spouse. If you plan ahead, there are some vegetables you can cook any time you have the oven on. Sweet potatoes or squash can be roasted while you are making roast chicken, for example. You can store the cooked veggies in the fridge until you are ready to puree or puree them right away. Spinach puree takes barely 5 minutes to make, so consider it a quickie option when you are especially short on time.

Prep and Cook the Vegetables

Cooking is where you need to be careful, because too much time on the stove will evaporate precious nutrients and too little time will make the pureeing difficult and the results a little grainy. As with equipment, it's important to choose the method that's easiest and most effective for you—experiment! Here's a review of the different ways I cook my veggies for purees.

STEAMING (all veggies)

1. Wash the vegetables and drain them in a colander.

2. Peel, trim, and cut up the vegetables as recommended on pages 196–197.

3. Put about 1 inch of water in the bottom of the pot. Add a steamer basket (without the vegetables), cover, and bring the water to a boil. (Or follow the instructions that come with your rice steamer.)
   If you don't have any other type of steamer, you also can steam in a saucepan. Bring ½ inch of water to a boil, add the veggies, cover, and steam. But be careful—the water evaporates quickly. If it does, the vegetables (and pan!) may burn.

4. Place the vegetables in the steamer—up to a double layer of veggies will steam well—cover, and steam the number of minutes recommended on pages 196–197.

5. Drain the vegetables in a colander.
   If you're steaming several different batches of vegetables, start each batch with fresh water. Particularly with green vegetables, the steaming water gets bitter, and it will turn the vegetables bitter too.

ROASTING (sweet potatoes and butternut squash)

1. Preheat the oven to 400°F.

2. Wash the vegetables and drain them in a colander.

3. Prepare the vegetables as indicated, unpeeled, and place them on a foil-lined baking sheet. Roast until tender.

4. Set the vegetables aside until cool enough to handle. Then scoop sweet potato or squash out of the peel with a tablespoon.

MICROWAVING (all veggies)

1. Wash the vegetables and drain them in a colander.

2. Peel, trim, and cut up the vegetables.

3. Put the vegetables in a glass or ceramic container. (No metal!) Add 2 tablespoons of water. Loosely cover with microwave-safe plastic wrap, a microwave-safe lid, or waxed paper.

4. Microwave in one-minute increments until the vegetables are tender when pierced with the tip of a sharp knife.

Puree

1. Put the veggies into a food processor or blender, secure the lid, press the "on" button ("grind" on a mini-food processor), and puree until smooth and creamy. Generally, this takes about two minutes.

   Puree large quantities in a standard-sized food processor; a mini-chopper works best for small quantities.

2. You may need to add a teaspoon or so of water to cauliflower, carrots, and broccoli to make a smooth, creamy puree.

3

Portion and Package the Purees

1. Measure the purees into ½-cup portions (sometimes I make ¼-cup portions, depending on the recipe) and package in small zipper-lock plastic bags if you plan to use the puree within a few days (or in freezer bags for longer storage). Many people have told me they use ice-cube trays. Whatever works for you is great! From time to time I'll use a muffin tin, but baggies work well for me most often.

2. Using a permanent marker, label each bag with the type and amount of puree and the date. For example, "½ cup squash, 6/27/10."

3. Refrigerate purees that will be used in the next couple of days; freeze the rest. I use plastic storage bins in both the fridge and the freezer to hold the bagged purees. The bags stay more organized, and it's easier to keep track of which ones to use first.

4

Cook

Now that you have your kitchen and pantry stocked, you're ready to use the recipes.

1. Scan the recipes and choose the purees you need. Always use older purees first (check the date).

2. Thaw bags of frozen puree in a bowl of hot tap water.

3. Snip the corner of the bag with scissors to squeeze out the puree for your recipe.

Vegetable Purees: How To

BROCCOLI

Prep: Cut into florets.

Cook: Steam for 6 to 7 minutes. Florets should be tender but still bright green. (If they're an olive green, they're overcooked.)

Puree: Use a food processor or blender for about 2 minutes. May need a few teaspoons of water, for a smooth, creamy texture.

BUTTERNUT SQUASH

Prep: Do not peel. Cut off stem, cut squash in half lengthwise and scrape out the seeds.

Cook: Roast the halves on a baking sheet, flesh-side down, in a 400°F oven for 45 to 50 minutes.

Puree: Scoop out the flesh and puree in a food processor or blender for about 2 minutes.

CARROTS

Prep: Peel, trim the ends, and cut into 3-inch chunks.

Cook: Steam for 10 to 12 minutes.

Puree: Use a food processor or blender for about 2 minutes, with a few teaspoons of water, for a smooth texture.

CAULIFLOWER

Prep: Cut off florets and discard the core.

Cook: Steam for 8 to 10 minutes.

Puree: Use a food processor or blender for about 2 minutes, with a few teaspoons of water if needed for a smooth, creamy texture.

SWEET POTATOES

....

Prep: Do not peel. Cut into quarters if
         steaming. Leave whole if roasting.

Cook: Steam for 40 to 45 minutes.
         Roast in a 400˚F oven for 50 to
         60 minutes.

Puree: Scoop out the flesh and puree in a
         food processor or blender.

SPINACH

....

Prep: No prep at all for baby spinach. For
         mature spinach, fold leaves in half
         lengthwise with the stem outside, then
         strip the stem off the leaf.

Cook: Steam for 30 to 40 seconds, or cook
         in a skillet with 1 tablespoon water for
         about 90 seconds, or just until wilted.

Puree: Use a food processor or blender
         for about 2 minutes, until smooth
         and creamy.

YELLOW SQUASH

....

Prep: Trim off the ends and cut into
         1-inch pieces.

Cook: Steam for 6 to 8 minutes.

Puree: Use a food processor or blender for
         about 2 minutes, until smooth.

The Skinny on Fats

So many people are concerned, rightfully so, with fats and oils in their food. It's such a confusing subject that I asked Lisa Sasson to weigh in: "Fat improves the taste and aroma of many foods. It's also an essential nutrient that provides many health benefits. In fact, we can't live without it! Adding a little fat—such as salad dressing or drizzling a little oil on your vegetables—helps your body absorb some of the vital nutrients. So a fat-free or very low-fat diet should NOT be a health goal.

Instead, the focus should be on consuming moderate amounts of healthy fats and to enjoy them instead of feeling guilty!" That sounds great to me, especially because I love the flavor of olive oil and enjoy full-fat cheese from time to time. I'm glad I can enjoy them without a lot of worry. Instead, I pay attention to my portion sizes.

Basically, to be a smarter food shopper, you should know about three types of fat: saturated fats, unsaturated fats, and trans fats.

SATURATED FAT is solid at room temperature and is found in animal products like butter, full-fat dairy products, meats, and in some vegetable oils, such as palm, palm kernel, and coconut oil. Most of us eat saturated fats every day in red meats and dairy products and such packaged goods as cookies, cakes, crackers, and dairy creamers. A little saturated fat is fine; diets high in saturated fats can raise bad cholesterol and may increase your risk of heart disease.

UNSATURATED FAT is liquid at room temperature and is classified in two categories: polyunsaturated and monounsaturated fats. These fats come from vegetable sources, so they contain no cholesterol (unlike most of the saturated fats, which come from animal sources). Replacing saturated fat in our diet with polyunsaturated and monounsaturated fats appears to have many health benefits.

Polyunsaturated fats appear in corn, safflower, soybean, sunflower, and sesame oils and in fish. Monounsaturated fats are in most nuts, peanut oil, sesame seed oil, canola oil, olive oil, and avocados. Saturated and unsaturated fats have the same number of calories, around 120 per tablespoon.

Omega-3 fatty acids are a type of polyunsaturated fat that are often singled out because they may help protect against heart disease and reduce inflammation, which is associated with heart disease, arthritis, and strokes. The best sources of omega-3 fatty acids come from fish, such as salmon, tuna, sardines, and herring. Nonfish sources of omega-3 fatty acids include walnuts, flaxseed, and some green vegetables, such as kale, spinach, and salad greens, and canola and soybean oils.

TRANS FAT. Trans fats appear to raise your blood cholesterol level more than any other fat. Although a very small amount of trans fat is found naturally in meat and dairy products, most trans fat that is of health concern is made through an industrial process called hydrogenation which changes oil to be more solid. Food manufacturers love this type of fat, also known as partially hydrogenated fat, because it makes baked goods crispy, oils and fats more spreadable, and extends the shelf life of processed foods. Unfortunately, our hearts don't!

The food label will reveal if there is trans fat in the product. It's mostly found in cookies, crackers, and other packaged baked goods and commercially fried foods like French fries and doughnuts. If you see "partially hydrogenated fat" near the top of the ingredients list or any grams of trans fat in the nutritional panel, look for an alternative product. Ultimately, the best way to avoid unhealthy trans fats is to eat fewer processed foods. Preparing your own food means you are less likely to include unhealthy fats in your diet.

BOTTOM LINE

A key to eating better is to reduce the amount of saturated fat in your diet and keep trans fats as low as possible. Replace fatty cuts of meat and full-fat dairy with lean cuts of meat and poultry, fish, low-fat dairy products, heart healthy fats like olive oil, canola oil, wheat germ, avocado, nuts and seeds, and of course plenty of fresh fruits and vegetables, whole grains, and beans.

Recipe Index

Puree Index

Shrimp Dumplings, 91
Skinny Egg Salad, 121
Summer Corn Fritters, 109
Turkey Meatloaf, 73

Pumpkin
Chicken and Biscuits, 59
Ginger Cookies, 168
Pumpkin Ravioli, 96

Spinach
Cherries Jubilee Brownies, 153
Chicken Enchiladas, 62
Chicken Parmesan, 64
Fig Bars, 169–70
Mint Chocolate Chip Ice Cream, 183
Whoopie Pies, 148

Sweet Potato
Caramel Corn, 185
Chicken and Biscuits, 59
Chicken Enchiladas, 62
Chicken Satay, 60
Cinnamon-Maple Quinoa, 30
Gnocchi, 99
Honey Mustard Chicken, 55
Lo Mein, 83
Macaroni and Cheese, 102
Meatball Subs, 77

Oatmeal Raisin Cookies, 172
Orange Beef, 78
Tomato Soup, 49

Yellow Squash
Chocolate Peanut Butter Pie, 147
Lemon Cream Cookies, 161
Maple Peanut Butter Fondue, 133
Mixed Berry Cobbler, 136

Acknowledgments

Special and endless thanks go to Jennifer Rudolph Walsh at WME, Mary Ellen O'Neill at HarperCollins, John Smallwood at Smallwood & Stewart, Amy Harte and Merideth Harte Londagin at 3&Co, Jennifer Iserloh, Luc Turbier, Olivia Dupin, Tom Keaney, Joy Bauer, Lisa Sasson, Lisa Hubbard, Steve Vance, Anne Disrude, Deborah Williams, Orin (and Jeremy) Snyder, Larry Shire, Jonathan Ehrlich, Laura K. O'Boyle, Shelby Meizlik, Keleigh Thomas, Katherine Snider, the team at Baby Buggy, and the amazing Ricardo Souza.

Thanks to all the stores and shops, large and small, online and off, that were so very supportive of *Deceptively Delicious*. Not least, of course, I'm grateful to all my readers. From casual passersby to those of you who wrote or emailed, I truly appreciate your enthusiasm and support. I hope you find this book equally as helpful.

Finally, an enormous thank you goes to my husband and children, my grandmother, my parents, my sisters and their families, and many friends for tasting, re-tasting and weighing in on every recipe and detail of this book.